How To Teach

Front Crawl

Basic technique drills, step-by-step lesson plans and everything in-between

A swimming teacher's definitive guide to teaching front crawl swimming stroke

Mark Young

A Catalogue record for this book is available from the British Library

ISBN 9780995484214

Published by: Educate & Learn Publishing, Hertfordshire, UK

Graphics by Mark Young, courtesy of Poser V6.0

Design and typeset by Mark Young

Published in association with www.swim-teach.com

Note: This book is intended for guidance and support only. The material contained here should accompany additional course material set on an official swimming teaching course by an official Swimming Association. Neither the author nor the publisher can accept responsibility for any injury or loss sustained as a result of the use of this material.

Author Online!
For more resources and swimming help visit
Mark Young's website at

www.swim-teach.com

Swim Teach

Teaching · Learning · Achieving · Professional Swimming Help Online

Mark Young is a well-established swimming instructor with decades of experience of teaching thousands of adults and children to swim. He has taken nervous, frightened children and adults with a fear of water and made them happy and confident swimmers. He has also turned many of average ability into advanced swimmers. This book draws on his experiences and countless successes to put together this simplistic methodical approach to teaching swimming.

Also by Mark Young

Teaching Guides
How To Be A Swimming Teacher
101 Swimming Lesson Plans
How To Teach Breaststroke
How To Teach Backstroke
How To Teach Butterfly

Learn to Swim Guides
The Complete Beginners Guide to Swimming
How To Swim Front Crawl
How To Swim Breaststroke
How To Swim Backstroke
How To Swim Butterfly
The Swimming Strokes Book

Contents

Introduction

Swimming with good front crawl technique is a desire that many long for. Whether it is for competition, triathlon or just to get a sense of personal achievement, front crawl is the swimming stroke that most people want to know how to swim well.

What Makes A Good Teacher?

'A teacher is one who makes himself progressively unnecessary.'
Thomas Carruthers

What makes a good teacher?

A teacher is looked up to by their pupils as a role model and a source of knowledge and guidance. A teacher possesses several key characteristics that make him or her individual and it is these personal characteristics that can determine a teacher's level of success.

A good swimming teacher requires a wide range of qualities. You will probably be stronger in some areas than others and as you gain experience you will build your competence in all areas.

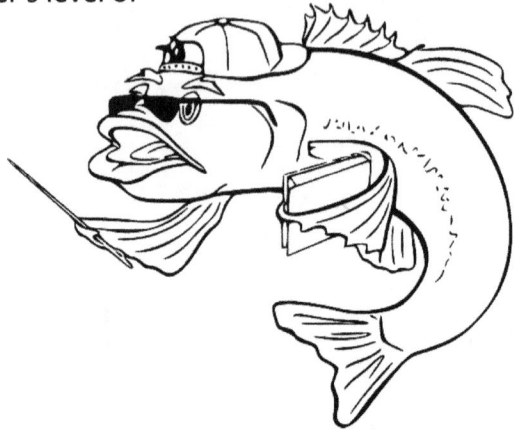

Teaching Qualities

To be a good teacher and role model to your pupils, you need to possess some essential qualities. These are:

Knowledge

Having sound knowledge of your subject gains you respect, not only from your pupils but from parents and other swimming teachers. You will need to keep your knowledge up to date and always admit when you don't know the answer, but make it your business to find out.

Empathy

Teaching swimming requires empathy on all levels. For example, the child who is scared and has every reason to be, the adult who is equally scared or even embarrassed, the child who is over-excited at the prospect of going in the pool and the child who is trying hard but not keeping up with the rest.

Patience

All of the above examples that require empathy will also test your patience. As a teacher, you have to accept that not everybody learns at the same rate. Children's behaviour and attention spans will also try your patience at times. Whatever is thrown at you, you must show patience and control at all times.

Control and Management

It goes without saying that you must have control over your class, especially with children in a pool. In the classroom at school, children know what is expected of them but this is not always the case in the swimming pool. Children have to be controlled for safety purposes as well as learning purposes.

If pupils are being unruly throughout the lesson then not only is the lesson unsafe, but they are not learning anything. The golden rule is to set out your stall early on to show them who is boss. That is not to say that you have to 'rule with fear', otherwise pupils will not want to have swimming lessons with you, just let those that step out of line know they have done so and that it will not be tolerated.

Effective Communication

As a teacher, your job is to pass on information effectively and clearly, and your ability to do this will determine how quickly your pupils learn. Knowledge of your subject is also essential, but how you convey that knowledge is far more important. You could be a world expert on the human body and the scientific principles behind swimming but if you are not able to pass that expertise onto eager-to- learn pupils clearly and concisely, then you are not a good teacher!

Basic Principles of Effective Communication

Positioning

Where you position yourself on the poolside will determine how well your pupils can see and hear you. Study the pool diagrams in the planning and organisation section for best practice.

Clarity

Passing information on clearly will ensure your pupils do exactly what you want them to.

Conciseness

Keep your teaching concise to avoid your pupils becoming confused or taking in the wrong pieces of information.

Accuracy

Your teaching has to be accurate as you will be copied, mimicked and quoted especially by children. Inaccuracy will result in your pupils not learning and in you gaining a reputation as a poor teacher.

Enthusiasm

A sure way to motivate your class and get results is to have an enthusiastic approach. Enthusiasm is infectious and if you are full of it when you teach, your pupils will put every effort into what you ask them to do.

Interest

If the content of what you teach is not interesting then your pupils will not listen and become distracted. Enthusiasm and interesting content go hand in hand, as one breeds the other. The most uninteresting subject can be made interesting with an injection of enthusiasm.

Appropriateness

The teaching points and practices you use will determine the success and outcome of the lesson. If your methods are not appropriate, the pupils do not learn and the lesson becomes pointless.

Two-way

Communication works both ways. Ask your pupils questions and listen carefully to those who answer and how they answer. Encourage them to ask you questions at appropriate times.

Motivation

As a teacher, you are also a motivator. Some pupils you teach will need more motivation than others. Most children can't wait to get into the pool and start swimming and impress the teacher.

You will, however, come across children who have swimming lessons because they have been made to do so by their parents, whether they need them or not. Either way, a motivating teacher brings out the best in pupils.

Praise

This is the easiest, most common form of motivation. Remember to praise effort as well as success.

Feedback

This is a more detailed, constructive form of praise. The pupils are given a clearer picture of how they are performing and improving. If feedback is to be motivational it has to be positive.

For example, a swimmer returns to the poolside after practising front crawl leg kick unsuccessfully. Your job is to teach and motivate them. Your feedback should go something like this:

'Well done, that was a good try' (praise for the effort)
'You were pointing your toes, which is good, well done.' (positive feedback)
'Try again, and this time kick your legs from your hips.' (feedback in the form of a teaching point)
Avoid negative feedback, for example, *'Don't bend your legs.'*

Teaching Adults

Adults will arrive on the poolside in all shapes and sizes and with differing levels of confidence. One thing that they will all have in common, however, is that they will all appreciate a relaxed and informal approach to being taught to swim.

Teaching adults how to swim front crawl brings its own set of barriers and limitations. These include:

Lack of Flexibility

Generally speaking, adults lack flexibility all over, so when it comes to swimming front crawl the main area that requires a large degree of movement are the shoulders. As a result, their arm action can often be quite limited. Arm pulls might be shortened, recovery over the water is often wide with much less of an elbow bend and hand and arm entry can lack a stretch forward.

The other area that adults often lack flexibility is in their ankles. This can affect the leg kick by preventing the feet and toes from pointing as they kick, which in turn can make the overall kick inefficient and cause drag. A lack of movement in the ankles also means a loss of the relaxed flipper-like action as they kick.

These lack of flexibilities often make for a very inefficient swimming stroke.

Lack of Fitness

Whilst a lack of general fitness and stamina is not always the case for adults in the swimming pool, learning to swim front crawl could be a relatively new challenge, so it is fair to say they lack 'swimming fitness'. They could be a regular marathon runner or accomplished long-distance cyclist, but still be completely exhausted after swimming one length of front crawl. This is very common.

Add together these two most common limitations and you have what most swimming teachers experience when teaching adults to swim - very slow progress.

Slow progress in adults learning to swim is completely normal and should not be looked upon negatively.

As a swimming teacher, there are a few things you can do to help.

- Be calm, relaxed and informal in your teaching style. This will help to relax your adult and keep them at ease.
- Adjust your expectations accordingly.
- Take their limitations into account when planning. Exercises and drills that suit one swimmer may not work for another.
- Be flexible in your approach. For example, fins or hand paddles (usually used in advanced drills) can often be beneficial to adult beginners, as long as they do not become reliant on them.
- Be sensitive to their frustrations and always show empathy and be supportive in your response.
- Above all, use plenty of praise to stimulate and maintain motivation. At the end of each lesson, pick out the parts they showed progress and highlight them as achievements of the session however small they may be.

Equipment

Equipment

Floats and kickboards

When used correctly swimming floats can help develop specific parts of your technique. They are suitable for non-swimmers right up to advanced swimmers and can be used by both adults and children.

Swim floats are used by swimming teachers as part of lessons for many different exercises. They can be used by non-swimmers to strengthen and by established swimmers to isolate and perfect technique.

For example, the weak non-swimmer can use two floats, one placed under each arm, to help strengthen their leg kick. The floats will provide stability and help boost confidence, whilst encouraging a fast and furious leg kick.

Advantages:

- Very versatile and can help enhance a wide range of swimming exercises.
- Can be used in addition to other aids.
- Can be used in place of other types of swimming aid to encourage progression and enhance strength and stamina.
- When used individually floats can help gain leg or arm strength.
- Fine-tune technique by encouraging a swimmer to focus on a certain area of their swimming stroke.
- Cheap to buy and easy to store. Also easy to use with large groups.

16

Disadvantages:

- Not suitable for very young children or babies learning to swim as they require a degree of strength to hold.
- Require close supervision

Common Mistakes to Watch Out For

It's difficult to use a float incorrectly because they are such a simple piece of swimming equipment. However, there are a couple of points to watch out for when using floats to teach children.

Firstly, it is common for children to grip the float too tightly, especially if they are a nervous beginner. They squeeze the float in their hand, resulting in a very tired hand grip and the focus away from the part of their swimming they are supposed to be concentrating on.

Secondly, it is common for children to bare their weight onto the float, causing it to submerge. Once again this is easily done by the nervous beginner as they attempt to climb above the water surface instead of laying on the surface. Reassuring them and helping them to relax by advising them to "let the float support you", will go some way to helping children to get the most out of swimming floats.

These common problems can take time to fix as the swimmer begins to learn how to relax and become comfortable in the water. As long as the teacher aware and the swimmer is made aware, then gradual progress can be made.

Woggle or Noodle

One of the most popular buoyancy aids, the swimming noodle, is a simple polythene foam cylinder. One of the most popular and widely used floats during swimming lessons.

Sometimes called a 'woggle', it is cheap to make, cheap to buy and easy to use in large group swimming lessons.

The main advantage is that it provides a high level of support whilst at the same time allowing the swimmer movement of their arms and legs. The swimmer can learn and experience propulsion through the water from both the arms and the legs.

The noodle is very versatile and as it is not a fixed aid, it can be used and removed with ease. It can also add a sense of fun to swimming as it can be tucked under the arms on the front and the back as well as placed between the legs and used as a 'horse'. The noodle is ideal for beginners learning breaststroke technique.

Advantages and Disadvantages of a Swimming Noodle

Advantages:

- Provides a high level of support for children of all sizes.
- Gives a sense of independence in the water with the minimum of support.
- Allows freedom of movement.
- Boosts confidence in the nervous beginner.
- Able to support adult beginners
- Easy to fit and remove, so ideal for use in group swimming lessons.
- Allows freedom of movement.

Disadvantages:

- Limited or no use for advanced swimmers.
- Nervous swimmers can 'clamp' it between their body and their arms, restricting their arm action.
- Can cause very buoyant swimmers to tip forwards.

Pull Buoy

A pull buoy is a figure-eight shaped piece of solid foam and used mainly by established and advanced swimmers.

It is placed between the legs in the upper thigh area to provide support to the body so the swimmer can swim without kicking the legs. This allows them to focus on other parts of their swimming stroke, such as arm technique or breathing technique.

This type of swimming aid is most useful when learning and practising front crawl and backstroke swimming techniques.

These training aids are most commonly used by competitive swimmers during their training sessions. They are designed to restrict the use of the swimmer's lower body, causing a greater intensity on the arms and upper body.

The nature of holding it between the legs by squeezing the thighs together also helps to keep the lower body in a streamlined and efficient shape during the swim. By isolating the upper body, the swimmer can focus completely on their arm or breathing technique, whilst the float assists to keep the lower body afloat.

They also help to strengthen the upper body and arms by eliminating the kick propulsion, while helping to keep the body position correct in the water.

This type of swimming aid is available in a smaller size for younger swimmers as well as full size for adults.

Pull Buoy Advantages and Disadvantages

Advantages:

- Provide good isolation of the upper body whilst keeping the lower body buoyant.
- Ideal for work-outs and training and therefore for established and advanced swimmers.

- Increased core strength
- Available in adult and junior sizes

Disadvantages:

- Not suitable for non-swimmers and beginners.

Sinkers

Sinkers are objects such as sticks, hoops and toys that sink to the bottom of the pool. They are a great way to teach children breath control by encouraging them to submerge.

Sinkers can be used in both shallow and deep water and vary in design to cater for a range of ages. Although their uses rarely target a specific swimming stroke, they can open up a huge range of contrasting and complementary activities.

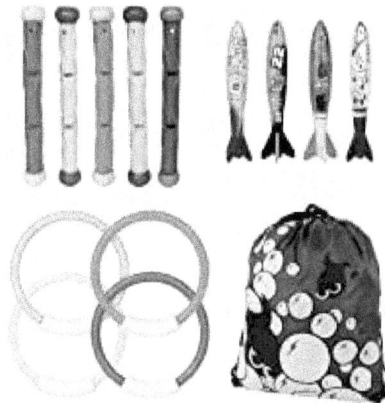

To children, sinkers are the equivalent of toys, so a swimming teacher with a creative imagination can use them to spark excitement and get some fantastic results.

Fins

For beginners learning to swim, swimming fins are a great way to help develop a correct kicking action for front crawl, backstroke and butterfly stroke. This is because they help to keep the feet and toes in a pointed position and they encourage the ankle and knee joints to be relaxed during the kicking action.

However swimmers and teachers must not become over-reliant on swimming flippers. They are useful for helping to build strength and power but swimmers should be encouraged to take them off and try to transpose the feeling into your feet by making your feet behave like flippers as you swim.

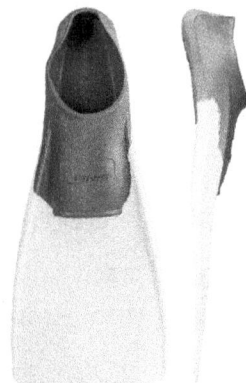

Hand Paddles

Hand paddles used to develop power in the arms, chest, shoulders and back muscles. They come in the form of large plastic paddles that strap to the palms of the hands and prevent the water from passing through the fingers.

The swimmer can use hand paddles to enhance their feel for the water and in that, in turn, will help to improve technique.

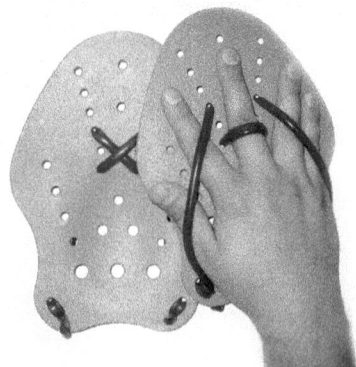

Front Crawl Technique

Front Crawl Technique

Front crawl is the fastest, most efficient stroke of them all. This is largely down to the streamlined body position and continuous propulsion from the arms and legs. The alternating action of the arms and legs is relatively easy on the joints and the stroke as a whole develops aerobic capacity faster than any other stroke. In competitive terms, it is usually referred to as Freestyle.

The constant alternating arm action generates almost all of the propulsion and is the most efficient arm action of the four basic swimming strokes. The leg action promotes a horizontal, streamlined body position and balances the arm action but provides little propulsion.

Front crawl breathing technique requires the head to be turned so that the mouth clears the water but causes minimal upset to the balance of the body from its normal streamlined position.

The timing and coordination of the arms and legs occur most commonly with six leg kicks to one arm cycle. However, stroke timing can vary, with a four-beat cycle and even a two-beat cycle, which is most commonly used in long-distance swims and endurance events.

Body Position

The overall body position for front crawl is as streamlined and as flat as possible at the water surface, with the head in-line with the body.
The waterline is around the natural hairline with eyes looking forward and down.

If the position of the head is raised it will cause the position of the hips and legs to lower which in turn will increase frontal resistance, causing the stroke to be inefficient and the breathing technique to be incorrect.

If the head position is too low it will cause the legs to rise and the kick to lose its efficiency.

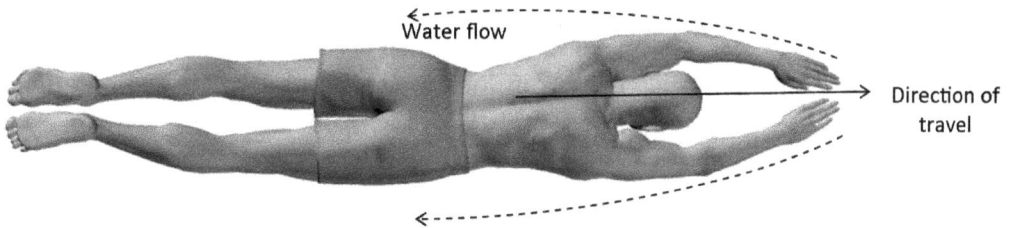

Water flow

Direction of travel

Streamlined body position minimises drag, allowing efficient movement through the water

Shoulders remain at the surface and roll with the arm action. Hips also roll with the stroke technique, close to the water surface and the legs remain in line with the body.

Common Body Position Mistakes

The common body position mistakes made are with head position and hand and feet position during the stroke.

If the head is too high over the water surface, it will cause the legs and feet to be lower under the water surface and cause the overall body position to be angled and therefore very inefficient.

Hands and feet must be together throughout the swimming stroke as this gives the body its streamlined efficiency, allowing it to move smoothly through the water. If the hands or feet move apart it causes the overall shape of the body in the water to become wider and therefore inefficient.

The best exercise to practice perfecting the correct body position and shape is a push and glide from the poolside. The swimmer pushes off from the pool wall or floor and glides across the water surface, keeping the head central and hands and feet touching together.

Leg Kick

The leg kick for front crawl originates from the hips and both legs kick with equal force.

The legs kick in an up and down alternating action, with the propulsive phase coming from the down kick. There should be a slight bend in the knee due to the water pressure, to produce the propulsion required on the down kick.

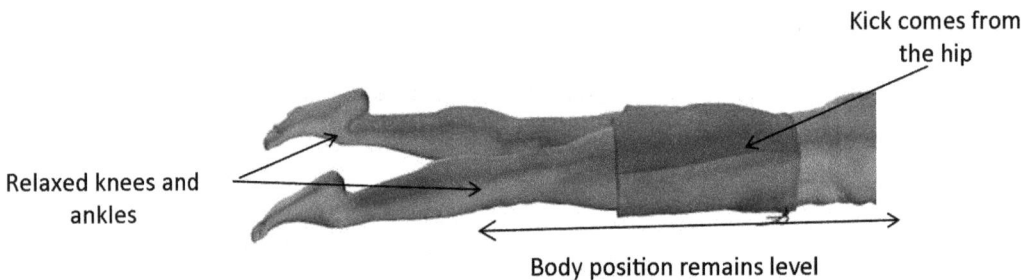

Kick comes from the hip

Relaxed knees and ankles

Body position remains level

The downward kick begins at the hip and uses the thigh muscles to straighten the leg at the knee, ending with the foot extended to allow it's surface area to bear upon the water. As the leg moves upwards, the sole of the foot and the back of the leg press upwards and backwards against the water.

The upward kick slows and stops as the leg nears and minimally breaks the water surface. Ankles are relaxed and toes pointed to give an in-toeing effect when kicking and the leg kick depth should be within the overall depth of the body.

Common Leg Kick Mistakes

It is very common to kick from the knees during front crawl, in an attempt to generate some propulsion and movement. This can also lead to a very stiff and robotic kicking action. The kick must originate from the hip and be a smooth movement with relaxed knee and ankle joints.

Another common mistake is to make the kicking movements too large. In other words, the feet come out over the water surface causing excessive splash and again wasting valuable energy.

A good exercise to practice the leg kick is holding a float or a kickboard and kicking along the length of the pool with face down. This will allow the swimmer to focus purely on the leg kick, ensuring it is a relaxed and flowing up and down movement.

Arms

The continuous alternating arm action provides the majority of the power and propulsion of the entire swimming stroke.

entry
The hand enters the water at a 45-degree angle, fingertips first, thumb side down. The hand entry should be between the shoulder and head line with a slight elbow bend.

catch
The hand reaches forward under the water without over-stretching and the arm fully extends just under the water surface.

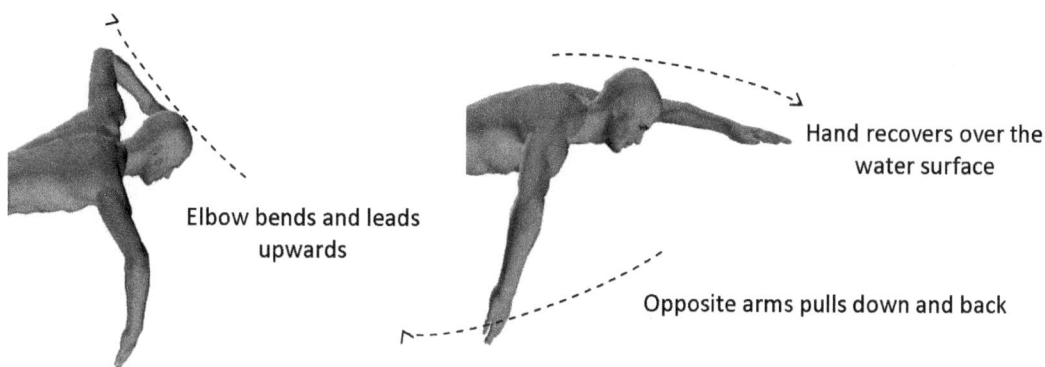

Elbow bends and leads upwards

Hand recovers over the water surface

Opposite arms pulls down and back

propulsive phase

The hand sweeps through the water downwards, inwards and then upwards. The elbow is high at the end of the down sweep and remains high throughout the in-sweep. The hand pulls through towards the thigh and upwards to the water surface.

recovery phase

The elbow bends to exit the water first. Hand and fingers fully exit the water and follow a straight path along the body line over the water surface. The elbow is bent and high and the arm is fully relaxed.

Common Arm Technique Mistakes

The arm action can bring about many mistakes, the most common being a deep propulsive phase and a very high recovery phase.

Both of these mistakes will disturb the body position, which will in turn create an inefficient overall swimming stroke. Both a deep arm pull and a high arm recovery over the water surface will also cause excessive body roll.

The best exercise for practising and correcting these common mistakes is holding a float in one hand and swimming using single arm pulls. This will force the swimmer to focus on the arm technique whilst ensuring that the body position remains level and correct.

Breathing

The head turns to the side on inhalation for front crawl breathing technique. The head begins to turn at the end of the upward arm sweep and turns enough for the mouth to clear the water and inhale. The head turns back into the water just as the arm recovers over and the hand returns to the water.

Breathing can be bilateral (alternate sides every one and a half stroke cycles) or unilateral (same side) depending on the stroke cycle and distance to be swum.

Types of Breathing Technique

Breath IN as the arm pulls through and the head turns to the side

Trickle Breathing

The breath is slowly exhaled through the mouth and nose into the water during the propulsive phase of the arm pull. The exhalation is controlled to allow inhalation to take place easily as the arm recovers.

Explosive Breathing

The breath is held after inhalation during the propulsive arm phase and then released explosively, part in and part out of the water, as the head is turned to the side.

Common Breathing Mistakes

It is very common, especially for beginners, to perform explosive breathing without knowing they are doing so. Holding the breath during the swimming stroke comes naturally to most people but it is not necessarily the most energy efficient way of swimming.

Breath holding causes an increase in carbon dioxide in the system, which increase the urgency to breathe. This can cause swimmers to become breathless very quickly.

Trickle breathing is the most effective breathing technique for beginners as it allows a gentle release of carbon dioxide from the lungs, which then makes inhalation easier.

Another common mistake is to lift the head instead of rolling the head to the side. Lifting the head causes the legs to sink and the overall body position to be disturbed and the swimming stroke to be inefficient.

The best exercise for perfecting trickle breathing and ensuring the head is not lifting is to hold a float with a diagonal grip and kick. The diagonal grip allows space for the head to roll to the side.

Timing

The timing and coordination for front crawl usually occur naturally.
The arms should provide a powerful propulsive alternating action whilst leg kicks also remain continuous and alternating.

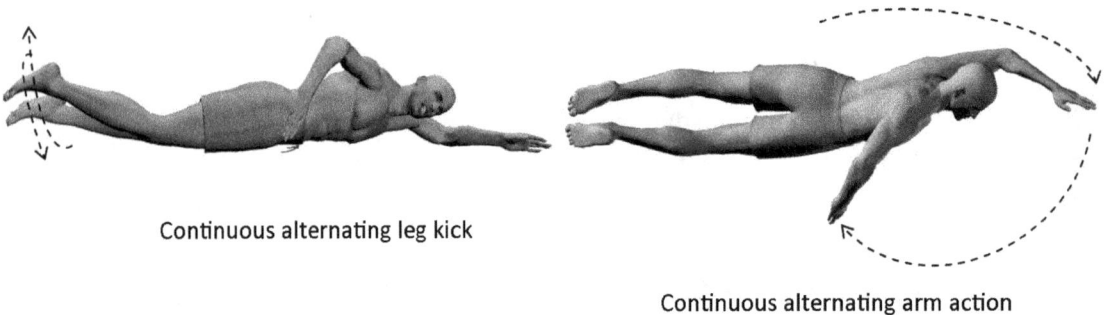

Continuous alternating leg kick

Continuous alternating arm action

However, there are a few variations.

Six beat cycle – each leg kicks three down kicks per arm cycle. The cycle is normally taught to beginners and used for sprint swims.
Four beat cycle – each leg kicks down twice for each arm pull.

Two-beat cycle – each leg kicks one downbeat per arm cycle. Long distance swimmers normally use this timing cycle, where the leg kick acts as a counterbalance instead of a source of propulsion.

Common Mistakes

These various timing and coordination cycles bring varying degrees of mistakes, the most common being an attempt to kick too fast.

The required speed of the leg kick and therefore the timing cycle required for the stroke depends on the distance that is to be swum. A long distance swim requires the leg kick to counterbalance the arm action, so the two-beat cycle is best used. The short sprint requires a faster leg kick so the six-beat cycle is needed so that the legs can provide more propulsion.

It is easy to kick with a fast leg kick and unknowingly allow the arm action to also speed up. This results in a loss of arm technique and overall body shape leading to a poor and inefficient swimming stroke.

Catch up is the best swimming exercise to not only establish correct timing and coordination cycle but to experiment with different timing cycles, as the delayed arm action slows down the exercise.

Front Crawl Exercises

**'I hear and I forget
I see and I remember
I do and I understand'**
Confucius

Front Crawl Exercises

The lessons plans that follow on from these exercises cover lessons for beginners, intermediate and advanced swimmers. Although these exercises form the foundation from which to teach front crawl, many other exercises are used throughout the lesson plans.

Every swimming teacher has their own 'take' on a particular exercise and many will have more exercises and drills in their repertoire to call upon. Listing all possible front crawl exercises and drills and their variations would be an endless task and therefore beyond the scope of this book.

It is assumed that a swimming teacher will use their professional judgement and experience to make the best use of the exercises and lesson plans outlined here.

Body Position

Holding the poolside

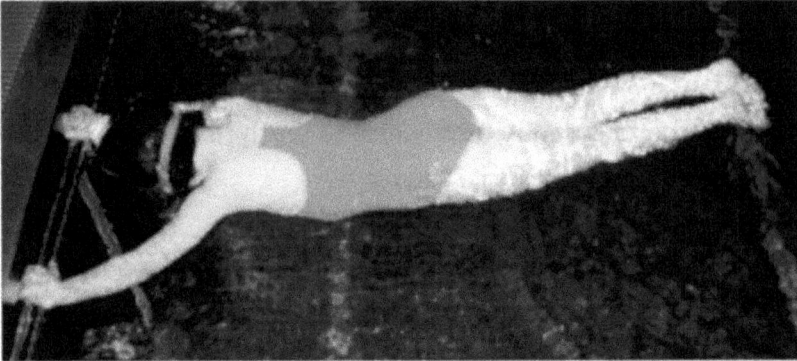

Aim: to encourage confidence in a floating position.

The pupil holds the poolside for added security and some assistance may be required, as some pupils will not naturally float.

Teaching Points

- Relax
- Keep the head tucked between the arms
- Stretch out as far as you can
- Keep your feet together
- Shoulders should be level

Teacher's Focus

- Head is central and still
- Face is submerged
- Eyes are looking downwards
- Hips are close to the surface
- Legs are together and in line with the body

Body Position
Holding the poolside

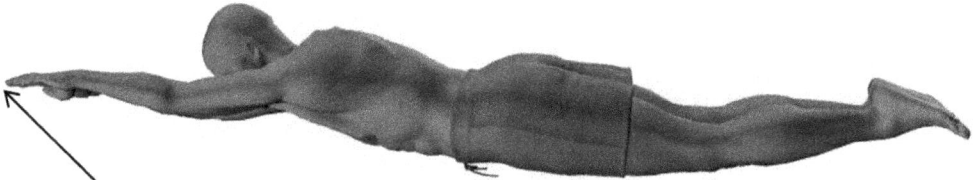

Hands holding the
poolside or rail

Overall body position is as horizontal as possible,
depending on the swimmers own buoyancy.

Common Faults	Remedy
Failure to submerge the face	Revert to previous exercises to build confidence
Head is not central	Reiterate the teaching point and demonstrate
Whole body is not remaining straight	Reiterate the teaching point and demonstrate
Feet and hands are not together	Reiterate the teaching point and demonstrate

Body Position

Static practice holding floats

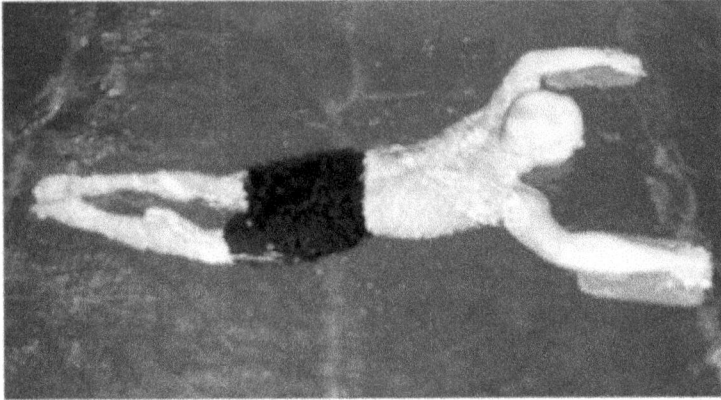

Aim: to help the swimmer develop confidence in his/her own buoyancy.

A float can be held under each arm or a single float held out in front, depending on levels of confidence and ability. Some swimmers may need extra assistance if they lack natural buoyancy.

Teaching Points

- Relax
- Keep the head tucked between the arms
- Stretch out as far as you can
- Keep your feet together

Teacher's Focus

- Head is central and still
- Face is submerged
- Eyes are looking downwards
- Shoulders should be level
- Hips are close to the surface
- Legs are together and in line with the body

Body Position
Static practice holding floats

Overall body position is horizontal and as flat as possible

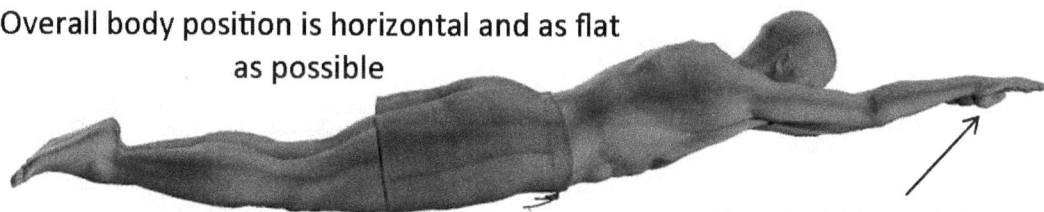

Float held in each hand or single float held in both hands

Common Faults	Remedy
Failure to submerge the face	Revert to previous exercises to build confidence
Head is not central	Reiterate the teaching point and demonstrate
Whole body is not remaining straight	Reiterate the teaching point and demonstrate
Feet and hands are not together	Reiterate the teaching point and demonstrate

Body Position

Push and glide from standing

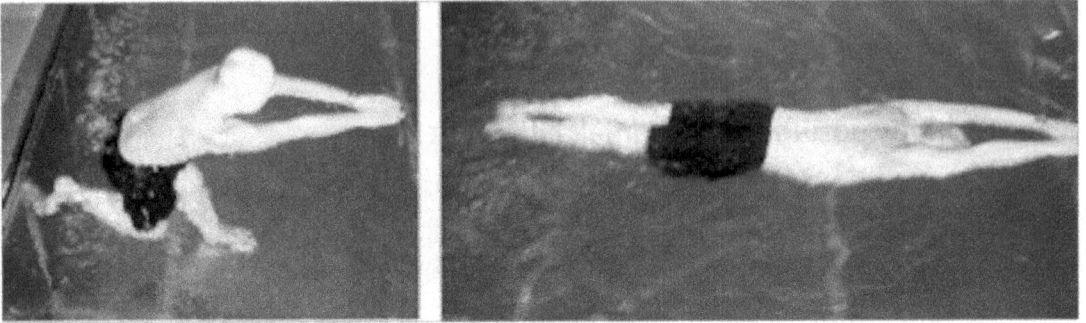

Aim: to develop correct body position and confidence in pushing off.

The swimmer can start with arms stretched out in front and pushes off from the pool floor or from the wall with one foot and glides through the water unaided.

Teaching Points

- Push hard from the side/pool floor
- Keep your head tucked between your arms
- Stretch out as far as you can
- Keep your hands together
- Keep your feet together

Teacher's Focus

- Initial push should be enough to gain good movement
- Head remains still and central
- Face submerged so that the water is at brow level
- Shoulders should be level
- Legs in line with the body

Body Position
Push and glide from standing

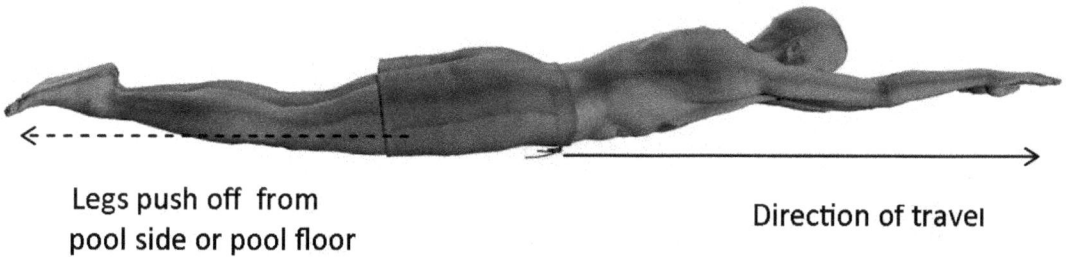

Legs push off from
pool side or pool floor

Direction of travel

Common Faults	Remedy
Failure to submerge the face	Revert to previous exercises
Push off is too weak	Reiterate the teaching point and demonstrate
Whole body is not remaining straight	Reiterate the teaching point and demonstrate
Feet and hands are not together	Reiterate the teaching point and demonstrate

Body Position

Push and glide from the side holding floats

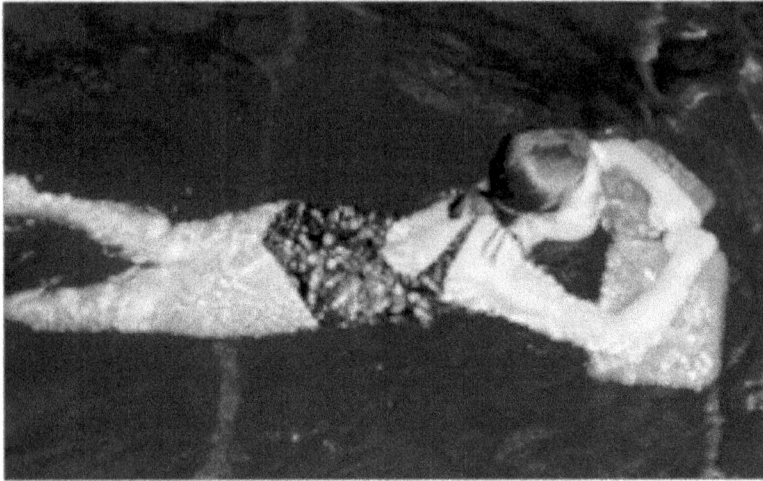

Aim: to develop correct body position whilst moving through the water.

Body position should be laying prone with the head up at this stage. The use of floats helps to build confidence, particularly in the weak or nervous swimmer. The floats create a slight resistance to the glide, but this is still a useful exercise.

Teaching Points

- Push hard from the wall
- Relax and float across the water
- Keep your head still and look forward
- Stretch out as far as you can
- Keep your feet together

Teacher's Focus

- Head remains still and central with the chin on the water surface
- Eyes are looking forwards and downwards
- Shoulders should be level and square
- Hips are close to the surface
- Legs are in line with the body

Body Position
Push and glide from the side holding floats

Water flow

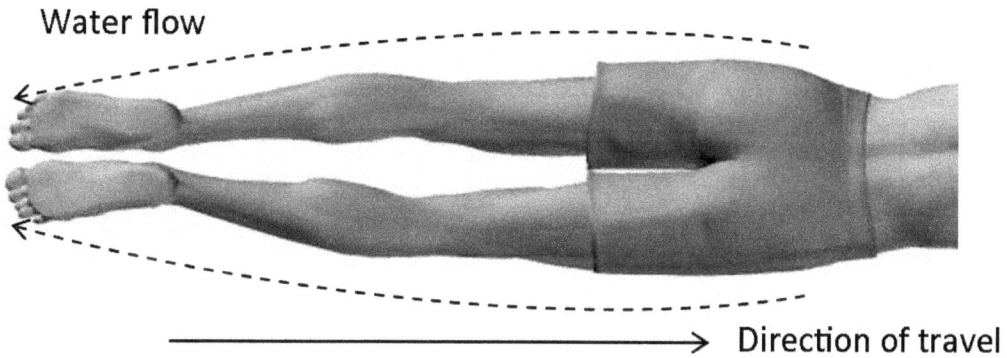

Direction of travel

Common Faults	Remedy
Push from the side is not hard enough	Revert to previous exercises
Head is not central	Reiterate the teaching point and demonstrate
Whole body is not remaining straight	Reiterate the teaching point and demonstrate
Feet are not together	Reiterate the teaching point and demonstrate

Body Position

Push and glide from the poolside

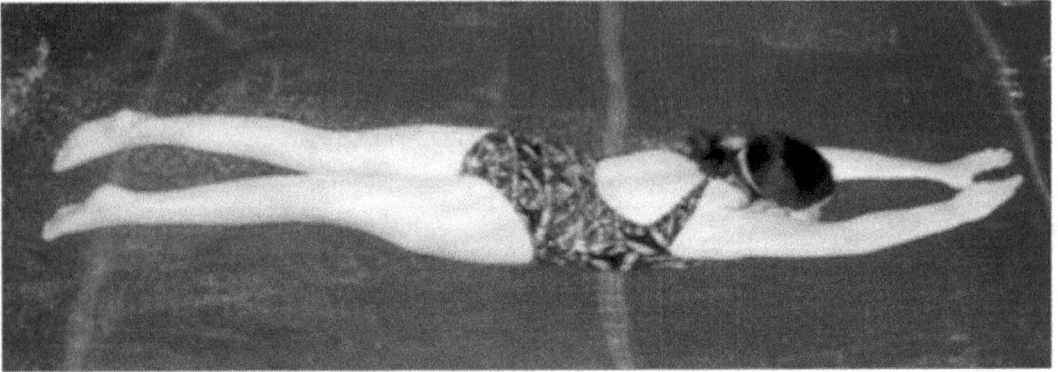

Aim: to develop a streamlined body position whilst moving thorough the water.

Movement is created by pushing and gliding from holding position at the poolside.

Teaching Points

- Head remains still and central
- Face submerged so that the water is at brow level
- Shoulders should be level and square
- Legs are in line with the body
- Overall body position should be streamlined

Teacher's Focus

- Push hard from the side
- Stretch your arms out in front as you push
- Keep your head tucked between your arms
- Stretch out as far as you can
- Keep your hands and feet together

Push and glide from the poolside

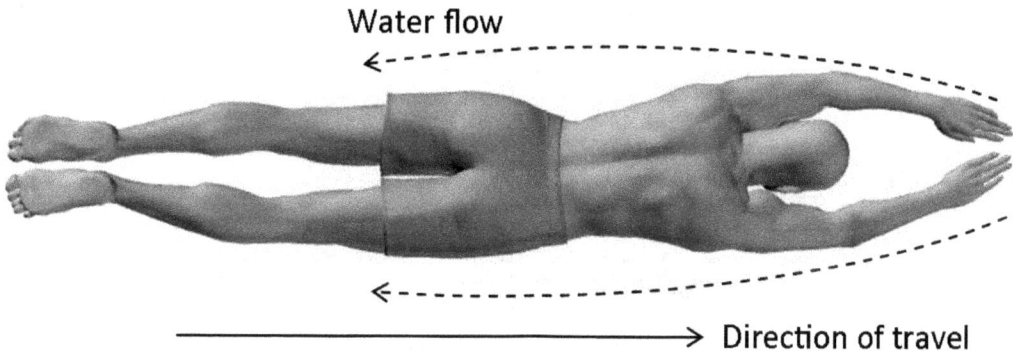

Water flow

Direction of travel

Streamlined body position minimises drag, allowing efficient movement through the water

Common Faults	Remedy
Push from the side is too weak	Reiterate the teaching point and repeat
Arms stretch in front *after* the push	Standing practice with arms in front
Head is not central	Reiterate the teaching point and repeat
Feet are not together	Reiterate the teaching point and demonstrate
Overall body position not in line	Revert to the previous exercise

45

Legs

Sitting on the poolside kicking

Aim: to give the swimmer the feel of the water during the kick.

Sitting on poolside kicking is an ideal exercise for the beginner to practise correct leg kicking action with the added confidence of sitting on the poolside.

Teaching Points

- Kick with straight legs
- Pointed toes
- Make a small splash with your toes
- Kick with floppy feet
- Kick continuously

Teacher's Focus

- Kick is continuous and alternating
- Knee is only slightly bent
- Legs are close together when they kick
- Ankles are relaxed and the toes are pointed

Legs
Sitting on the poolside kicking

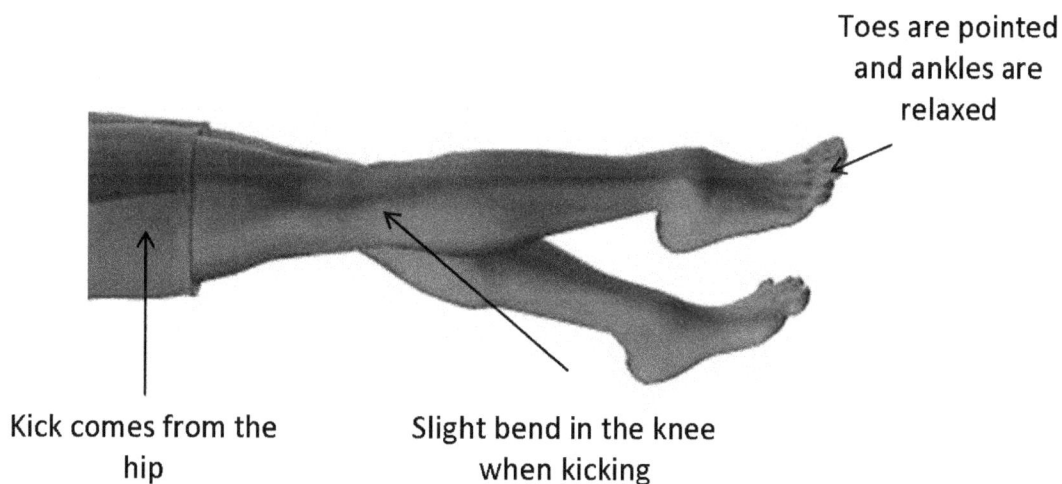

Toes are pointed and ankles are relaxed

Kick comes from the hip

Slight bend in the knee when kicking

Common Faults	Remedy
Knees bend too much	Reiterate the teaching point, demonstrate and practice
Kick comes from the knee	Reiterate the teaching point, demonstrate and practice
Ankles are not relaxed	Reiterate the teaching point, demonstrate and practice

Legs

Holding the poolside

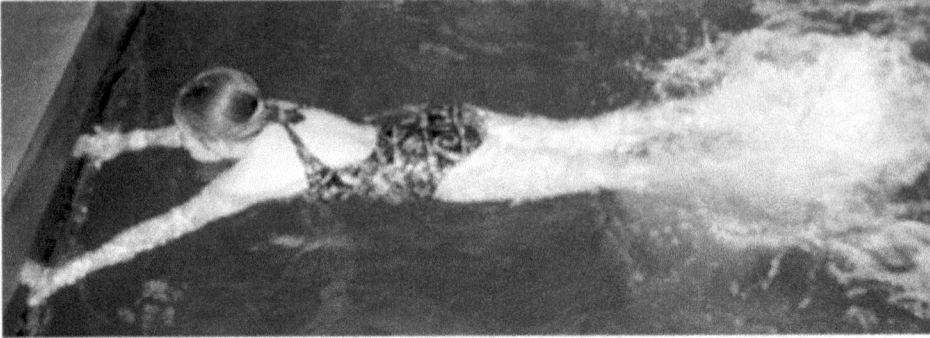

Aim: to encourage the swimmer to learn the kicking action.

Holding the poolside enhances confidence and helps develop leg strength and technique.

Teaching Points

- Kick with straight legs
- Pointed toes
- Make a small splash with your toes
- Kick with floppy feet
- Kick from your hips
- Kick continuously
- Legs kick close together

Teacher's Focus

- Kick comes from the hip
- Kick is continuous and alternating
- Knee is only slightly bent
- Legs are close together when they kick
- Ankles are relaxed and the toes are pointed
- Kick should just break the water surface

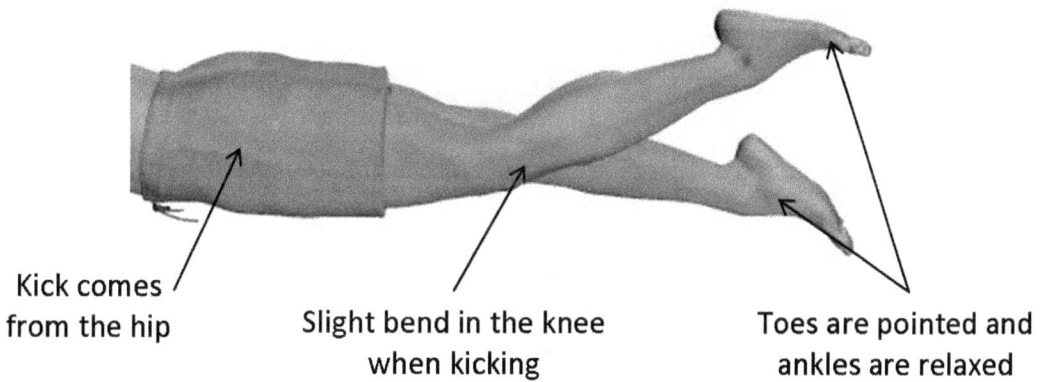

Kick comes from the hip

Slight bend in the knee when kicking

Toes are pointed and ankles are relaxed

Common Faults	Remedy
Feet come out of the water	Check the body position and repeat
Kick comes from the knee	Reiterate the teaching point, demonstrate and practice
Legs are too deep in the water	Check the body position and correct

Legs

Legs kick with a float held under each arm

Aim: to learn correct kicking technique and develop leg strength.

The added stability of two floats will help boost confidence in the weak swimmer.

Teaching Points

- Kick with straight legs
- Pointed toes
- Kick with floppy feet
- Kick from your hips
- Kick continuously

Teacher's Focus

- Kick comes from the hip
- Kick is continuous and alternating
- Chin remains on the water surface
- Legs are close together when they kick
- Ankles are relaxed and the toes are pointed
- Kick should just break the water surface
- Upper body and arms should be relaxed

Legs

Legs kick with a float held under each arm

Toes are pointed to provide streamline effect and ankles are relaxed

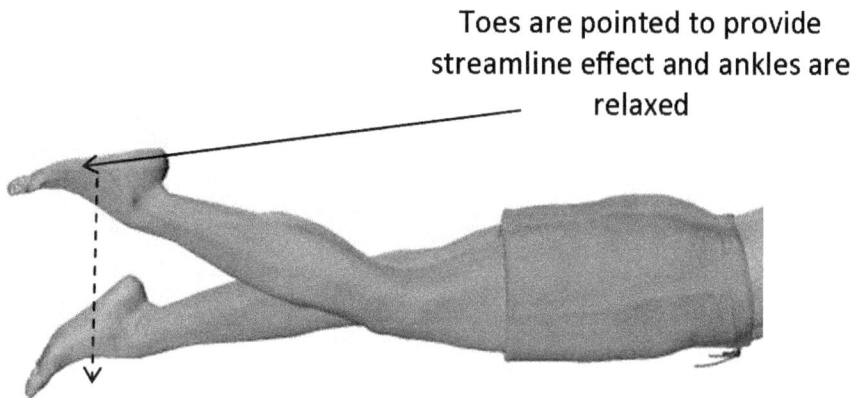

Downward kick provides propulsion

Common Faults	Remedy
Head lifts above the surface, causing the legs to sink	Encourage face submersion
Kick comes from the knee causing excessive bend	Reiterate the teaching point or revert back to a previous exercise
Kick is not deep enough	Encourage kicking from the hips
Legs are too deep in the water	Check the body position and correct

Legs

Float held with both hands

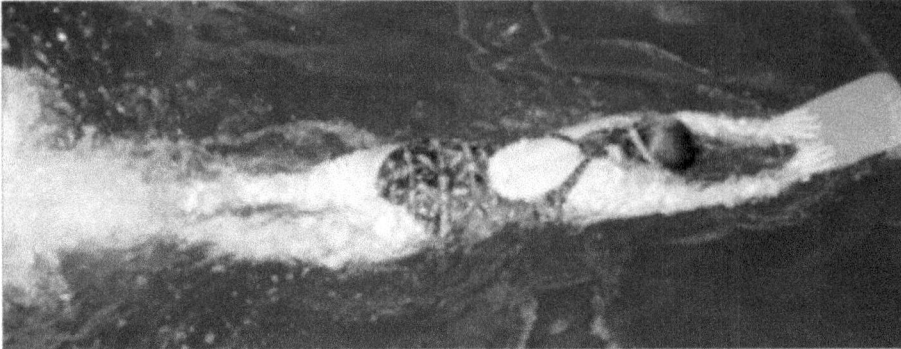

Aim: to practise and learn correct kicking technique.

Holding a float or kickboard out in front isolates the legs, encourages correct body position and develops leg strength.

Teaching Points

- Kick with pointed toes
- Make a small splash with your toes
- Kick with floppy feet
- Legs kick close together

Teacher's Focus

- Kick comes from the hip
- Kick is continuous and alternating.
- Legs are close together when they kick
- Ankles are relaxed and the toes are pointed.
- Kick should just break the water surface

Toes are pointed to provide streamline effect and ankles are relaxed

Downward kick provides propulsion

Knee is relaxed and slightly bent

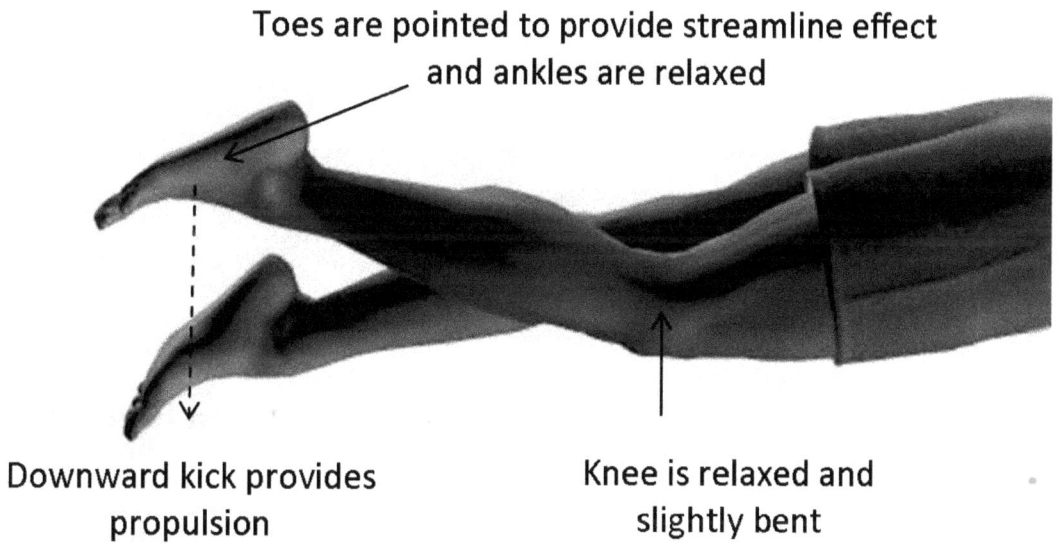

Common Faults	Remedy
Knees bend too much	Revert to earlier leg practices
Feet come out of the water	Check the body position
Kick comes from the knee	Reiterate the teaching point, demonstrate and practice
Legs are too deep in the water	Revert to earlier body position practices

Legs

Push and glide with added leg kick

Aim: to develop correct body position and leg kick whilst holding the breath.

Push and glide without a float and add a leg kick whilst maintaining a streamlined body position.

Teaching Points

- Kick with straight legs and pointed toes
- Kick with floppy feet
- Kick from your hips
- Kick continuously

Teacher's Focus

- Kick comes from the hip
- Streamlined body position is maintained
- Kick is continuous and alternating
- Legs are close together when they kick
- Ankles are relaxed and the toes are pointed
- Kick should just break the water surface

Legs
Push and glide with added leg kick

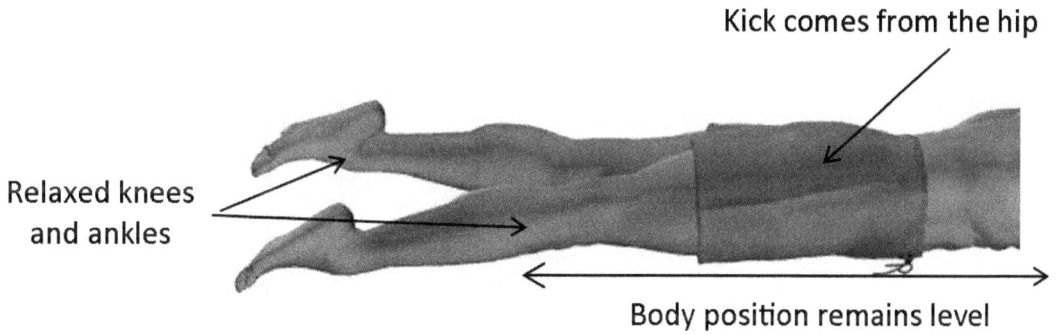

Kick comes from the hip

Relaxed knees
and ankles

Body position remains level

Common Faults	Remedy
Ankles are not relaxed	Revert to earlier leg practices
Feet come out of the water	Check the body position or revert to earlier exercises
Kick is not deep enough	Reiterate the teaching point, demonstrate and practice
Legs are too deep in the water	Revert to earlier body position practices

Legs

Leg kick whilst holding a float vertically in front

Aim: to create resistance and help develop strength and stamina.

Holding a float vertically in front increases the intensity of the kicking action, which in turn develops leg strength and stamina.

Teacher's Focus

- Kick with straight legs and pointed toes
- Kick with floppy feet
- Kick from your hips
- Kick continuously

Teaching Points

- Kick comes from the hip
- Streamlined body position is maintained
- Kick is continuous and alternating
- Legs are close together when they kick
- Ankles are relaxed and the toes are pointed
- Kick should just break the water surface

Legs
Leg kick whilst holding a float vertically in front

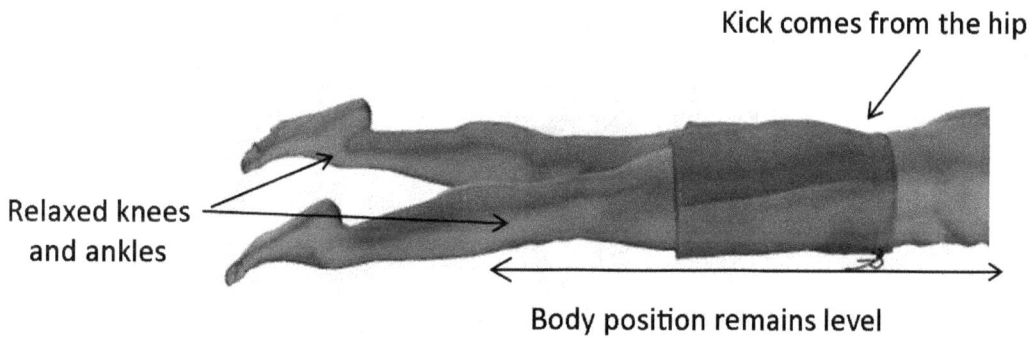

Kick comes from the hip

Relaxed knees
and ankles

Body position remains level

Common Faults	Remedy
Ankles are not relaxed	Revert to earlier leg practices
Feet come out of the water	Check the body position or revert to earlier exercises
Kick is not deep enough	Reiterate the teaching point, demonstrate and practice
Legs are too deep in the water	Revert to earlier body position practices

Arms

Standing on the poolside or in shallow water

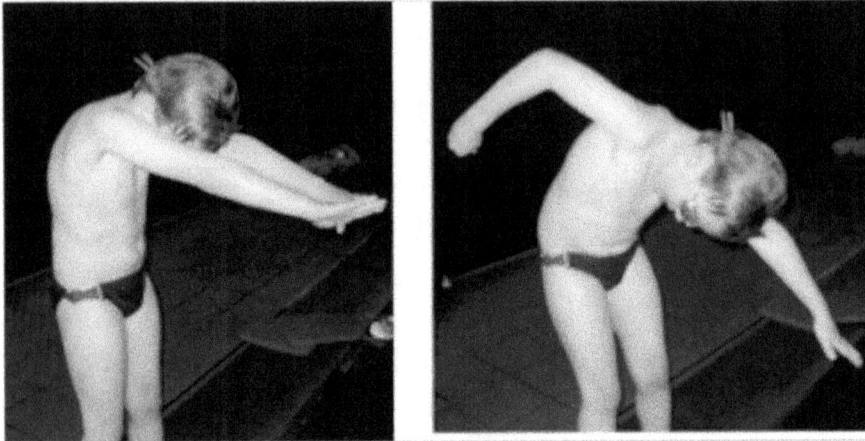

Aim: to practise correct arm movement whilst in a static position.

This is an exercise for beginners that can be practised on the poolside or standing in shallow water.

Teaching Points

- Keep your fingers together
- Continuous smooth action
- Brush your hand past your thigh
- Gradually bend your elbow

Teacher's Focus

- Fingers should be together
- Pull through to the hips
- Elbow bends and leads upwards

Arms

Standing on the poolside or in shallow water

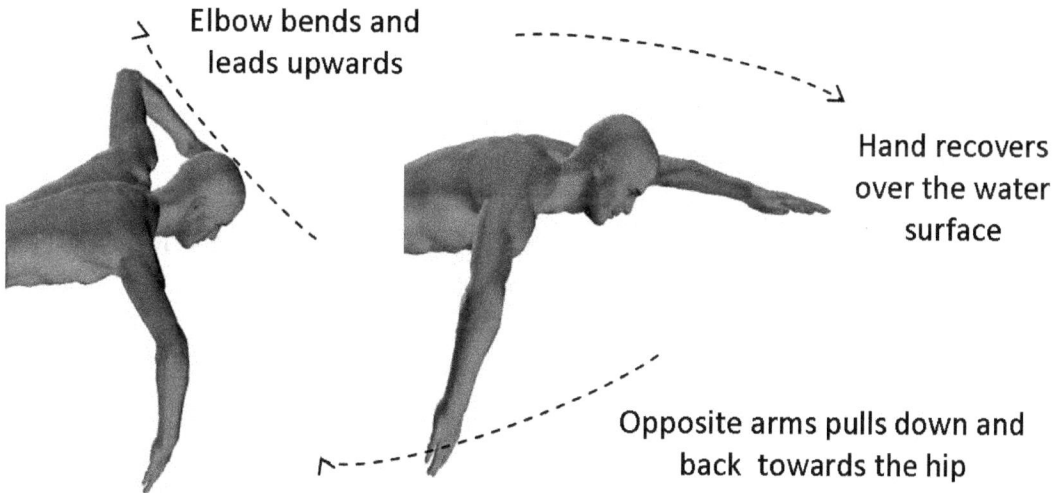

Elbow bends and leads upwards

Hand recovers over the water surface

Opposite arms pulls down and back towards the hip

Common Faults	Remedy
Fingers are too wide apart	Reiterate the teaching point, demonstrate and practice
Pull is short and not to the thigh	Encourage a longer pull
Arms are too straight as they pull	Encourage an elbow bend
Arms are too straight on recovery	Encourage an elbow bend
Hand entry is wide of the shoulder line	Reiterate the teaching point, demonstrate and practice

Arms

Single arm practice with float held in one hand

Aim: to practise and improve correct arm technique.

This practice allows the swimmer to develop arm technique whilst maintaining body position and leg kick. Holding a float with one hand gives the weaker swimmer security and allows the competent swimmer to focus on a single arm.

Teaching Points

- Keep your fingers together
- Brush your hand past your thigh
- Pull fast under the water
- Make an 'S' shape under the water
- Elbow out first
- Reach over the water surface

Teacher's Focus

- Fingertips enter first with thumb side down
- Fingers should be together
- Pull should be an elongated 'S' shape
- Pull through to the hips
- Elbow exits the water first
- Fingers clear the water on recovery

Single arm practice with float held in one hand

Elbow leads out of the water first

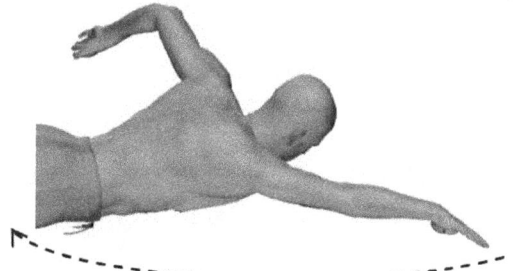

Arm pulls back through the water towards the hip

Common Faults	Remedy
Fingers are too wide apart	Reiterate the teaching point, demonstrate and practice
Pull is short and not to the thigh	Revert to the previous arm practice
Lack of power in the pull	Further arm exercises to build strength and stamina
Arm pull is too deep underwater	Revert to the previous arm practice
Arms are too straight on recovery	Repeat the static standing practice

Arms

Alternating arm pull whilst holding a float out in front

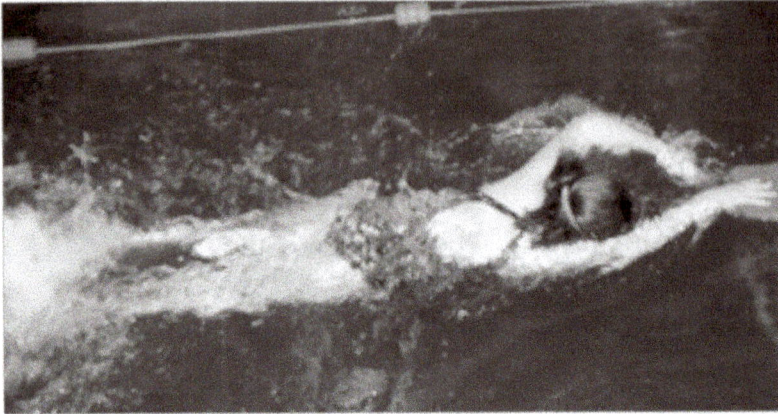

Aim: to develop coordination and correct arm pull technique.

The swimmer uses an alternating arm action. This also introduces a timing aspect, as the leg kick has to be continuous at the same time.

Teaching Points

- Finger tips in first
- Brush your hand past your thigh
- Pull fast under the water
- Elbow out first
- Reach over the water surface

Teacher's Focus

- Clean entry with fingertips first and thumb side down
- Fingers should be together
- Each arm pulls through to the hips
- Elbow leads out first
- Fingers clear the water on recovery

Arms
Alternating arm pull whilst holding a float out in front

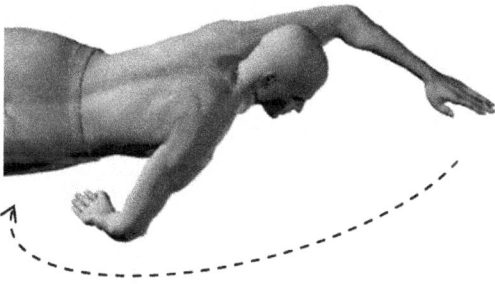

Arm pulls through towards the hip

Elbow leads high and the hand follows over the water surface

Common Faults	Remedy
Fingers are too wide apart	Reiterate the teaching point, demonstrate and practice
Pull is short and not to the thigh	Revert to the previous arm practice
Lack of power in the pull	Further arm exercises to build strength and stamina
Hand entry is wide of shoulder line	Revert to the previous arm practice
Arms are too straight on recovery	Repeat the static standing practice

Arms

Arm action using a pull-buoy

Aim: to develop arm pull strength, technique and coordination.

This is a more advanced exercise, which requires stamina and a degree of breathing technique.

Teaching Points

- Long strokes
- Smooth continuous action
- Brush your hand past your thigh
- Make an 'S' shape under the water
- Elbow out first
- Reach over the water surface

Teacher's Focus

- Fingertips enter first with thumb side down
- Fingers should be together
- Pull should be an elongated 'S' shape
- Pull through to the hips
- Elbow comes out first
- Fingers clear the water on recovery

Arm action using a pull-buoy

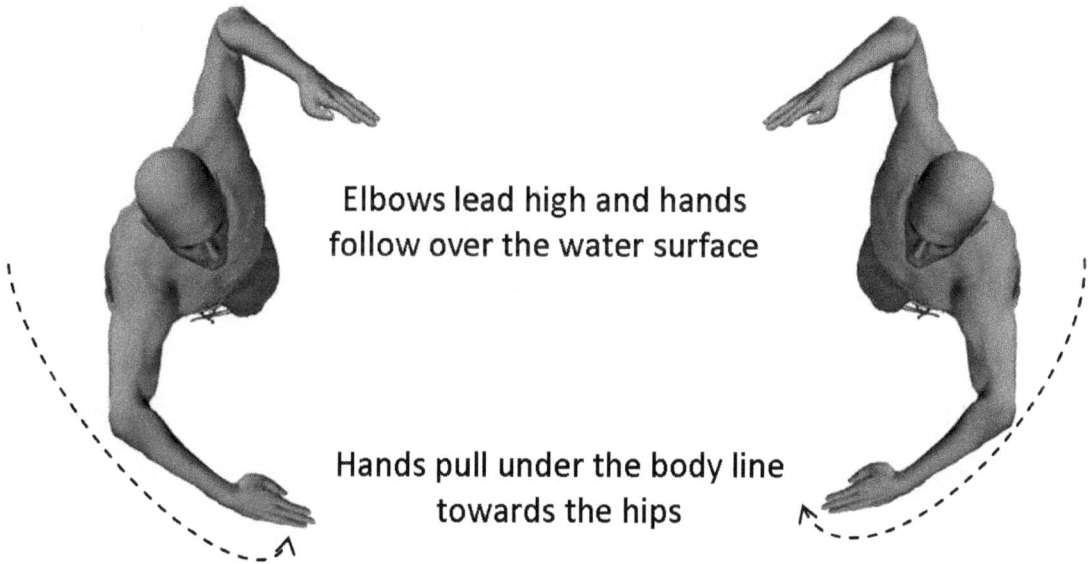

Elbows lead high and hands follow over the water surface

Hands pull under the body line towards the hips

Common Faults	Remedy
Arms pull too deep under water	Revert to the previous arm practice
Pull is short and not to the thigh	Revert to the previous arm practice
Lack of power in the pull	Further arm exercises to build strength and stamina
Hand entry is across the centre line	Repeat the earlier standing practice
Arms are too straight on recovery	Repeat the static standing practice

Arms

Push and glide adding arm cycles

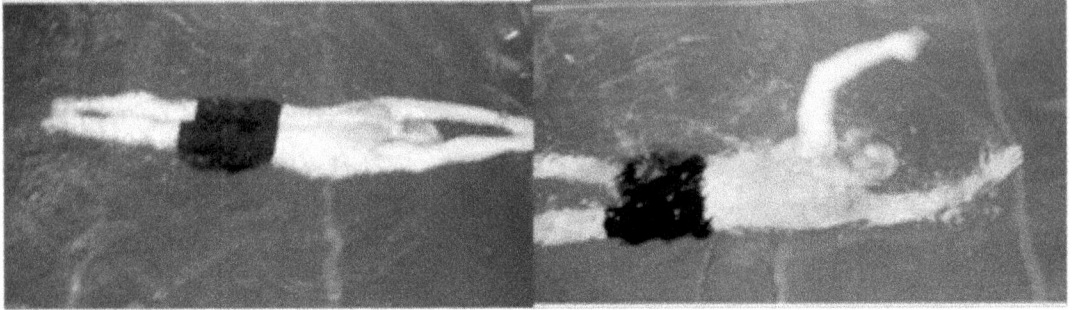

Aim: to combine correct arm action with a streamlined body position.

The swimmer performs a push and glide to establish body position and then adds arm cycles, whilst maintaining body position.

Teaching Points

- Finger tips in the water first
- Brush your hand past your thigh
- Make an 'S' shape under the water
- Elbow out first
- Reach over the water surface

Teacher's Focus

- Clean entry with fingertips first
- Pull should be an elongated 'S' shape
- Pull through to the hips
- Elbow comes out first
- Fingers clear the water on recovery

Arms

Push and glide adding arm cycles

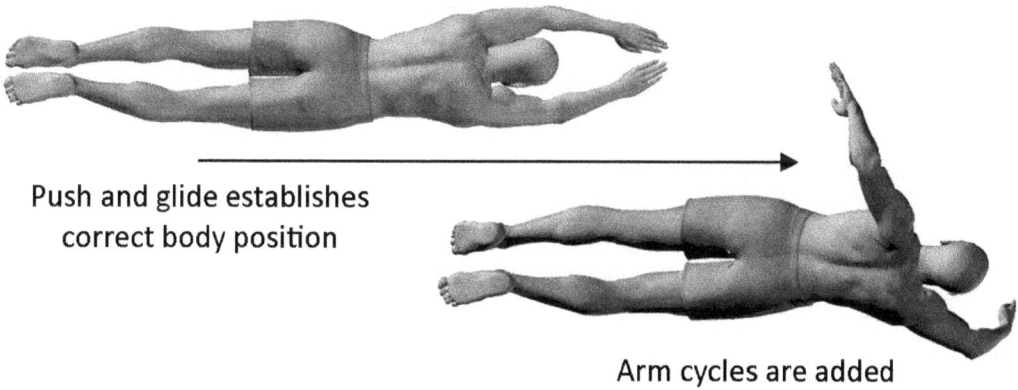

Push and glide establishes
correct body position

Arm cycles are added

Common Faults	Remedy
Arms are too straight under water	Reiterate the teaching point, demonstrate and practice
Pull is short and not to the thigh	Revert to the previous arm practice
Lack of power in the pull	Further arm exercises to build strength and stamina
Hand entry is across the centre line	Repeat the earlier standing practice
Arms are too straight on recovery	Repeat the static standing practice

Breathing

Standing and holding the poolside

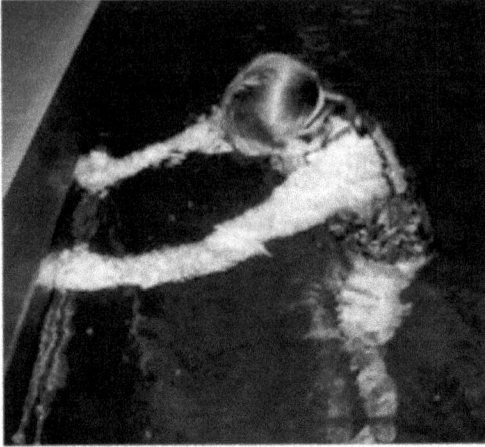

Aim: to practice and develop breathing technique.

The pupil stands and holds the pool rail with one arm extended, breathing to one side to introduce the beginner to breathing whilst having his/her face submerged.

Teaching Points

- Breathe out through your mouth
- Blow out slowly and gently
- Turn your head to the side when you breathe in
- See how long you can make the breath last

Teacher's Focus

- Breathing should be from the mouth
- Breathing in should be when the head is turned to the side
- Breathing out should be when the face is down

Breathing
Standing and holding the poolside

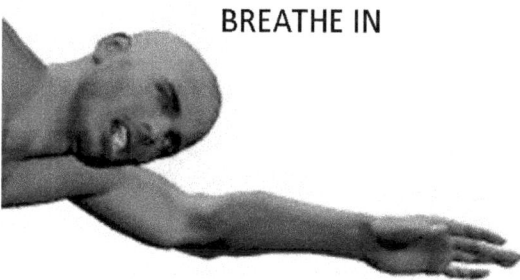

BREATHE IN

BREATHE OUT

Head turns to the side and mouth
clears the water surface

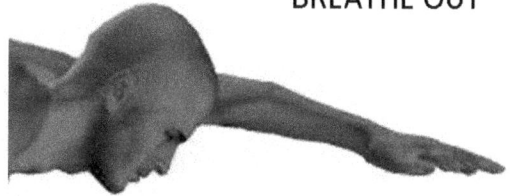

Head faces forward and down

Common Faults	Remedy
Breathing through the nose	Reiterate the teaching point, demonstrate and practice
Holding the breath	Revert to previous basic breathing exercises to encourage breathing out

Breathing

Holding a float in front with diagonal grip

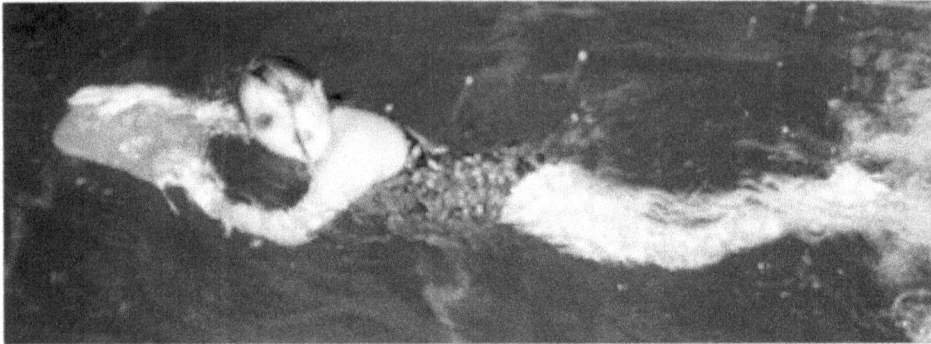

Aim: to encourage correct breathing technique whilst kicking.

The float is held in front; one arm extended fully, the other holding the near corner with elbow low. This creates a gap for the head and mouth to be turned in at the point of breathing.

Teaching Points

- Turn head towards the bent arm to breathe
- Breathe out through your mouth
- Blow out slowly and gently
- Return head to the centre soon after breathing

Teacher's Focus

- Breathing should be from the mouth
- Breathing in should be when the head is turned to the side
- Breathing out should be slow and controlled

Breathing
Holding a float in front with diagonal grip

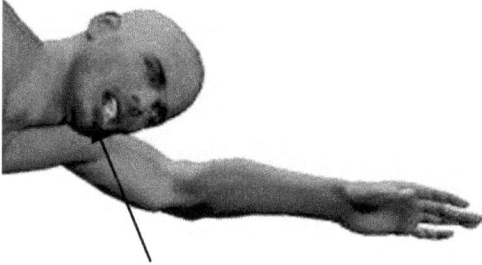

Breathe IN as the head turns
out of the water

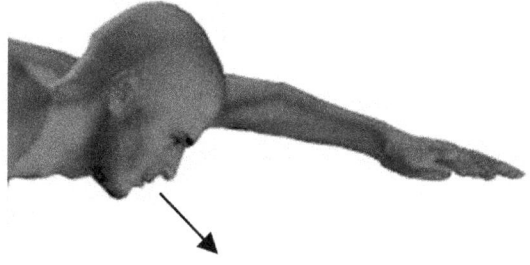

Breathe OUT as the head
faces forward and down

Common Faults	Remedy
Breathing through the nose	Reiterate the teaching point, demonstrate and practice
Holding the breath	Revert to previous basic breathing exercises to encourage breathing out
Lifting the head and looking forward	Reiterate the teaching point, demonstrate and practice
Turning towards the straight arm	Reiterate the teaching point, demonstrate and practice

Breathing

Float held in one hand, arm action with breathing

Aim: to develop correct breathing technique whilst pulling with one arm.

This allows the swimmer to add the arm action to the breathing technique and perfect the timing of the two movements. The float provides support and keeps the exercise as a simple single arm practice.

Teaching Points

- Turn head to the side of the pulling arm
- Breathe out through your mouth
- Blow out slowly and gently
- Return head to the centre soon after breathing

Teacher's Focus

- Head moves enough for mouth to clear the water
- Breathing in occurs when the head is turned to the side
- Breathing out should be slow
- Breathing should be from the mouth

Breathing

Float held in one hand, arm action with breathing

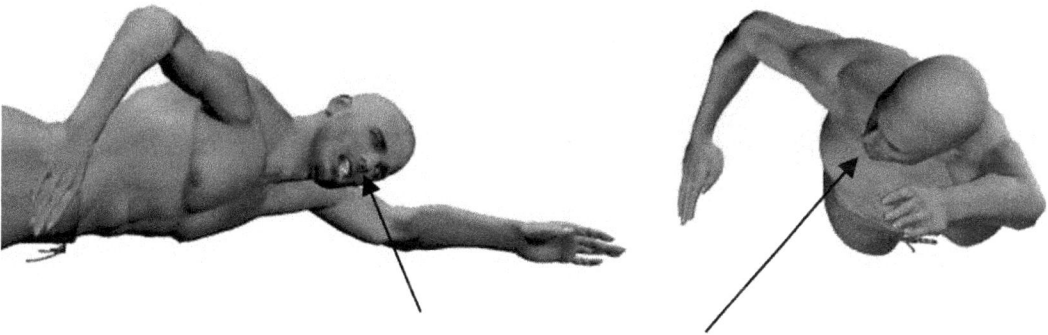

Breath IN as the arm pulls through and the head turns to the side

Common Faults	Remedy
Breathing through the nose	Reiterate the teaching point, demonstrate and practice
Holding the breath	Revert to previous basic breathing exercises to encourage breathing out
Lifting the head and looking forward	Revert to earlier breathing practices
Turning towards the straight arm	Revert to earlier breathing practices
Turning the head too much	Revert to earlier breathing practices

Breathing

Float held in both hands, alternate arm pull with breathing

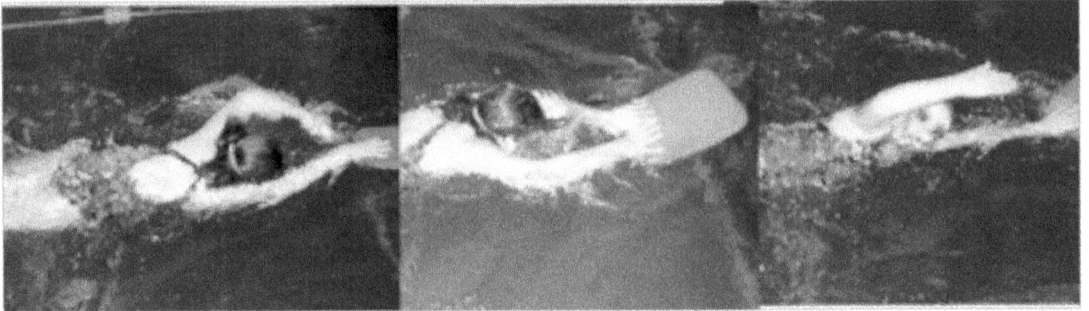

Aim: to practise bi-lateral breathing with the support of a float held out in front.

A single float is held in both hands and one arm pull is performed at a time with the head turning to breathe with each arm pull. Different arm action and breathing cycles can be used, for example; breathe every other arm pull or every three arm pulls.

Teaching Points

- Keep head still until you need to breathe
- Breathe every 3 strokes (or another pattern you may choose)
- Turn head to the side as your arm pulls back
- Return head to the centre soon after breathing
- Breathe out through your mouth

Teacher's Focus

- Head should be still when not taking a breath
- Head movement should be minimal enough for mouth to clear the water
- Breathing in should be when the head is turned to the side
- Breathing should be from the mouth

Breathing
Float held in both hands, alternate arm pull with breathing

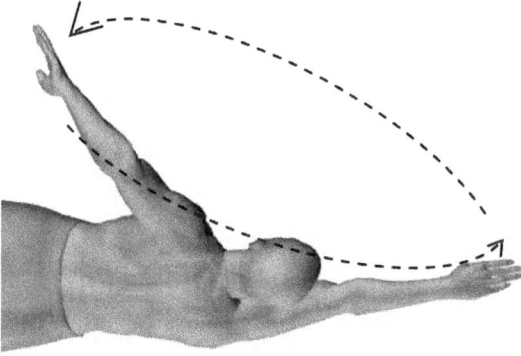

Head turns to the left side as the left arm pulls through and begins to recover

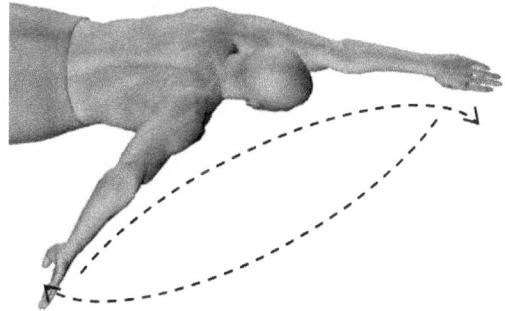

Head turns to the right side as the right arm pulls through and begins to recover

Common Faults	Remedy
Turning the head too early or late to breath	Reiterate the teaching point, demonstrate and practice
Lifting the head and looking forward	Revert to earlier breathing practices
Turning towards the straight arm	Revert to earlier breathing practices
Turning the head too much	Revert to earlier breathing practices

Timing

Front crawl catch up

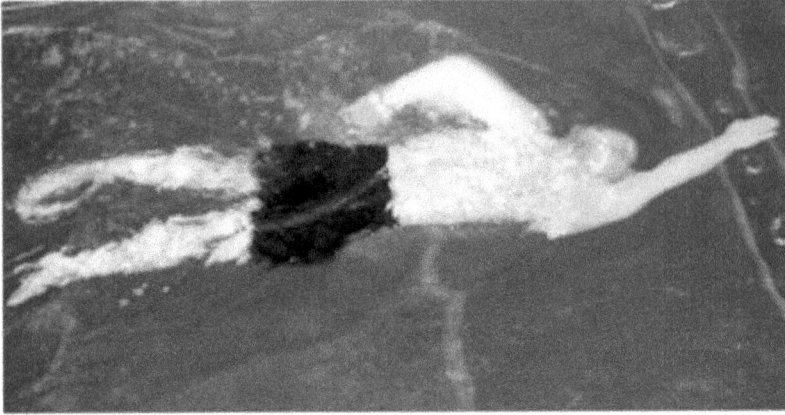

Aim: to practice correct stroke timing and develop coordination.

The opposite arm remains stationary until the arm performing the pull recovers to its starting position. This is an advanced exercise and encourages the swimmer to maintain body position and leg kick whilst practicing arm cycles.

Teaching Points

- Finger tips in the water first
- Brush your hand past your thigh
- Make an 'S' shape under the water
- Elbow out first
- Reach over the water surface

Teacher's Focus

- Clean entry with fingertips first
- Pull should be an elongated 'S' shape
- Pull through to the hips
- Elbow comes out first
- Fingers clear the water on recovery

Legs kick and
hands are held
together

One arm pulls and
recovers as the opposite
arm remains in front

Arm recovers to its position
in front before the opposite
arm pulls and recovers

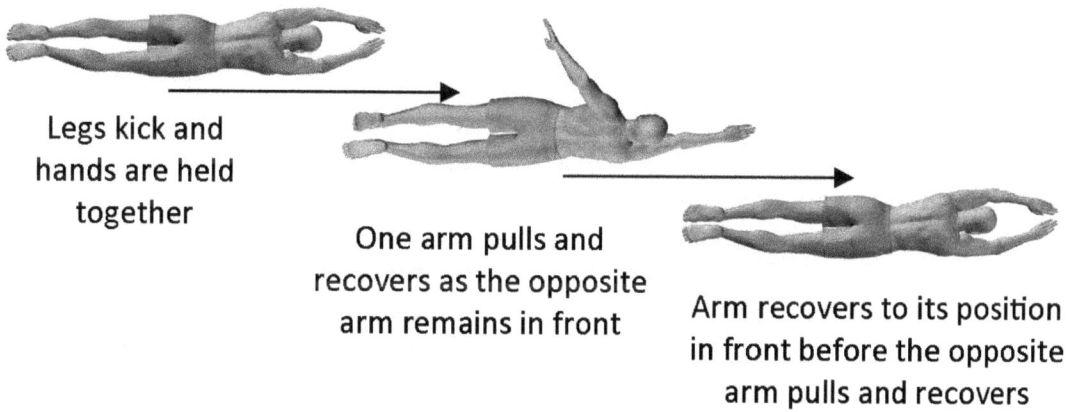

Common Faults	Remedy
Continuous leg kick but not enough arm pulls	Encourage rhythmic arm pull
Arm pull is too irregular	Encourage rhythmic arm pull

Full Stroke

Aim: full stroke Front Crawl demonstrating correct leg action, arm action, breathing and timing.

Teaching Points

- Keep your head still until you breathe
- Kick continuously from your hips
- Stretch forward with each arm action
- Pull continuously under your body
- Count 3 leg kicks with each arm pull

Teacher's Focus

- Stroke is smooth and continuous
- Head in line with the body
- Legs in line with the body
- Head remains still
- Leg kick is continuous and alternating
- Arm action is continuous and alternating
- Breathing is regular and to the side
- Stroke ideally has a 6 beat cycle

Common Faults	Remedy
Head moves from side to side	Revert to previous arm practices
Legs kick from the knee	Repeat earlier leg practices
Leg action is too slow	Repeat earlier leg practices
Arm action is untidy and splashing	Repeat earlier arm practices
Excessive head movement when breathing	Repeat previous breathing practices
Head is lifted, causing legs to sink	Repeat body position practices
Stroke is erratic and rushed	Check timing and encourage to swim slower

Lesson Plans

Lesson Plan Layout

Lesson Plan #2

Lesson type: full stroke front crawl

Level: adult or child intermediate

Previous learning: basic front crawl technique

Lesson aim: to progress and develop the whole stroke

Equipment: floats, pull buoys, sinkers and hoop

Lesson type: the part of front crawl that this lesson focuses on. For example, **Front Crawl Breathing Technique**.

Level: who the lesson is aimed at if they are beginners, intermediate or advanced level. For example, **Child Beginner.**

Previous learning: the aspects of swimming the pupil is expected to have covered before this lesson. For example, **basic front paddle**. The pupil is *not* expected to have completely mastered an aspect of swimming but should have had some experience of learning it.

Lesson aim: the lesson objective or desired outcome of the lesson. For example, 'to learn basic front crawl leg kick and introduce breathing'.

Equipment: the equipment you will need for this lesson. For example, 'floats, buoyancy aids and hoop'.

Lesson Sequences

Lesson plans are laid out in a sequence (beginner, intermediate, advanced) to give the teacher easy reference to other lessons, exercises and activities in the sequence. This should allow for easier differentiation across varying abilities.

Lesson plans do not have to be followed in sequence, although they can be if you wish. Each plan has its own aim and therefore can be used in sequence with other lessons aimed at that level, to suit the individual pupil or pupils.

These lesson plans and the exercises and activities in them are set out as a guide. Every pupil is different and will interpret and respond to exercises and teaching points in their own way, therefore as a swimming teacher it is important to be flexible in your approach. In other words, where a pupil is finding a particular exercise difficult, chose an easier exercise from a previous plan. Where a pupil is not quite grasping the concept of what you are teaching, try using a different phrase or teaching point.

Teaching Points

Teaching points are our 'magic words'. Having a variety of them in our virtual tool kit can be extremely useful. For example, when you say to a pupil 'point your toes and they just don't get it, you change the teaching point to 'kick with floppy feet'. All of sudden they are kicking with relaxed ankles and pointed toes.

Learning to be creative with our teaching points can be a very powerful skill and can be the difference between a pupil struggling and that light bulb moment when they suddenly understand and can do it.

Organising Your Swimmers

The way you chose to organise your swimmers as they swim off to perform a given exercise is vital to maintaining a safe learning environment and to monitor their progress.

The organisation column of the lesson plans make a suggestion but you will have to use your professional judgement, based on the size of your class and swimming lesson area available in your pool.

The suggestions are:

All together - you instruct all swimmers to go at the same time. Ideal if you have sufficient space and can be unsafe if you do not.

Waves - number your swimmers 1 and 2 alternately (or more if you have a large class). Then instruct all numbers 1's to go first, followed by the number 2's and so on if you have more. This is a good way of monitoring swimmers and also a great way to organise large classes of advanced swimmers.

One-by-one - sending each swimmer off one at a time. This is an ideal way to closely monitor each pupil.

Getting The Timing Right

All swimming pools vary in their dimensions and often larger pools have an area roped off for swimming lessons, so the whole pool is rarely used. These plans assume that beginner and intermediate swimmers will swim widths and advanced swimmers will swim lengths. The size of the width and length in *your* pool might not fit with how these plans are formatted and you may wish to use your professional judgment to change them to fit with your circumstances.

The duration of most swimming lessons is about 30 minutes. The timings of each exercise in these lesson plans are a guide and again, your professional judgement can be used to adjust them to suit your pupils and your pool size.

If you begin to discover that you are racing through the lesson and will have time left over, remember any exercise can be repeated. Repeating an exercise will enhance a pupil's strength, stamina and overall ability. A different teaching point can also be used to help those that perhaps did not quite get it the first time around.

Important Terminology:

Prone - 'facing downwards'. For example, a prone push and glide is performed in the face-down position.

Supine - 'facing downwards' For example, a supine star float is performed on the back, facing upwards.

Bi-lateral - 'both sides'. When referring to breathing technique, the swimmer is able to roll their head to both sides to take a breath.

'By failing to prepare
you are preparing to fail.'
Benjamin Franklin

Lesson Plan #1

Lesson type: full stroke front crawl stroke
Level: adult or child beginner
Previous learning: basic front paddle
Lesson aim: to learn each part of basic front crawl and experience the whole stroke
Equipment: floats, buoyancy aids and hoop

Exercise/Activity	Teaching Points	Organisation	Duration
Entry: swivel or steps entry	enter slowly	all together	1 min
Warm up: 2 widths any stroke with buoyancy aids if needed	take your time	all together	3 mins
Main Theme: push and glide, holding a float if needed	stretch out and glide	one by one	2 mins
kicking whilst holding a float under each arm	kick with floppy feet	all together	2 mins
single arm pull with a float held under one arm. repeat with opposite arm.	elbow leads out first	waves	4 mins
holding a float with a diagonal grip. repeat with head turning to the opposite side.	turn head to the bent elbow	waves	4 mins
alternate arm pulls holding float out in front	Count '1,2,3' each pull	waves	3 mins
full stroke front crawl	continuous arm pulls and leg kicks	waves	3 mins
Contrasting Activity: jumping entry and swim through a hoop	jump away from the side	2 or 3 at a time	3 mins
sitting dive through a hoop at the surface	head tucked down	2 or 3 at a time	3 mins
Exit: using the pool steps or over the poolside	take your time	one by one	1 min

Total time: 29 minutes

Lesson #1 Assessment

Lesson Objective: to learn each part of basic front crawl and experience the whole stroke.

Below average	Average	Above average
😐	🙂	😎
Attempts to demonstrate but does not show the correct technique	Able to perform most of the technique correctly some of the time	Performs the technique correctly most of the time

Assessment	😐	🙂	😎
Face in and out of the water as they move across the pool			
Kick leg is alternating			
Arms recover over the water surface			
Able to breathe without pausing			
Leg kicks and arm pulls are continuous			

Lesson Plan #2

Lesson type: full stroke front crawl

Level: adult or child intermediate
Previous learning: basic front crawl technique
Lesson aim: to progress and develop the whole stroke to an intermediate level
Equipment: floats, pull buoys, sinkers and hoop

Exercise/Activity	Teaching Points	Organisation	Duration
Entry: swivel or sitting dive entry	enter slowly	waves	1 min
Warm up: 2 widths any stroke	take your time	all together	3 mins
Main Theme: push and glide from the side	hands and feet together	one by one	2 mins
kicking whilst holding a float in both hands	kick with long legs	waves	3 mins
arms only using a pull buoy between the legs	pull and stretch	waves	3 mins
holding a float with a diagonal grip	breathe out slowly	waves	3 mins
push and glide, add arms pulls and leg kicks	continuous arm and legs	waves	3 mins
full stroke front crawl	steady and relaxed	waves	3 mins
Contrasting Activity: head first surface dives, collecting sinkers placed apart	deep breath and dig down	one by one	3 mins
dolphin kick through a hoop at the surface	swim like a mermaid	one by one	3 mins
Exit: using the pool steps or over the poolside	take your time	one by one	1 min

Total time: 28 minutes

Lesson #2 Assessment

Lesson Objective: to progress and develop the whole stroke to an intermediate level.		
Below average	**Average**	**Above average**
😐	🙂	😎
Attempts to demonstrate but does not show the correct technique	Able to perform most of the technique correctly some of the time	Performs the technique correctly most of the time

Assessment	😐	🙂	😎
Body position is horizontal			
Kick legs from the hips			
Kicks with toes pointed			
Finger and thumb enter the water first			
Head rolls to the side to breathe			
Leg kicks and arm pulls are alternating and continuous			

Lesson Plan #3

Lesson type: full stroke front crawl
Level: adult or child advanced
Previous learning: full stroke front crawl
Lesson aim: to develop and fine-tune technique for the whole stroke
Equipment: fins, pull buoys, hand paddles and floats

Exercise/Activity	Teaching Points	Organisation	Duration
Entry: sitting or shallow dive entry	take your time	waves	1 min
Warm up: 2 lengths front crawl	take your time	all together	3 mins
Main Theme: using fins, push and glide adding leg kicks	make your body long	waves	2 mins
kicking whilst holding a float vertically in the water	kick with floppy feet	waves	3 mins
full stroke using hand paddles	pull with power	waves	3 mins
using fins, front crawl breathing with increased time intervals	breathe out slowly	waves	3 mins
push and glide, add arms pulls and leg kicks	smooth, balanced strokes	waves	3 mins
full stroke front crawl	steady and relaxed	waves	3 mins
Contrasting Activity: dolphin kick underwater, arms by sides	lead with your head	one by one	3 mins
treading water	head above the water	waves	3 mins
Exit: using the pool steps or over the poolside	take your time	one by one	1 min

Total time: 28 minutes

Lesson #3 Assessment

Lesson Objective: to develop and fine-tune technique for the whole stroke.		
Below average	**Average**	**Above average**
😐	🙂	😎
Attempts to demonstrate but does not show the correct technique	Able to perform most of the technique correctly some of the time	Performs the technique correctly most of the time

Assessment	😐	🙂	😎
Body position is horizontal and streamlined			
Leg kick is relaxed and rhythmical			
Kicks with toes pointed and relaxed ankles			
Arms pull to the thighs and elbow exists first			
Arm recovery is controlled and not rushed			
Breathing is regular and without pause			
Stroke timing has a continuous 6 beat cycle			

Lesson Plan #4

Lesson type: front crawl body position
Level: adult or child beginner
Previous learning: basic front paddle and submerging the face
Lesson aim: to learn basic front crawl body position
Equipment: floats, buoyancy aids and hoop

Exercise/Activity	Teaching Points	Organisation	Duration
Entry: swivel entry	enter slowly	all together	1 min
Warm up: 2 widths any stroke using buoyancy aids	take your time	all together	3 mins
Main Theme: standing, holding the poolside and submerging	deep breath and relax	all together	2 mins
holding the poolside in a horizontal position and submerging face	arms out stretched	all together	3 mins
push and glide with floats under each arm	relax and glide	one by one	4 mins
push and glide with a float held in both hands	stretch out, point toes	all together	3 mins
push and glide without buoyancy aids	hands together	waves	2 mins
push and glide adding front crawl stroke	stretch out and relax	waves	3 mins
Contrasting Activity: submerging to collect an object	take your time	2 or 3 at a time	4 mins
tuck (mushroom) float	chin and knees to chest	all together	2 mins
Exit: using the pool steps or over the poolside	take your time	one by one	1 min

Total time: 28 minutes

Lesson #4 Assessment

Lesson Objective: to learn basic front crawl body position.		
Below average	**Average**	**Above average**
😐	🙂	😎
Attempts to demonstrate but does not show the correct technique	Able to perform most of the technique correctly some of the time	Performs the technique correctly most of the time

Assessment	😐	🙂	😎
Face is submerged			
Body position is flat			
Legs and feet are together			
Hands are together			
Hips are level			
Shoulders are level			

Lesson Plan #5

Lesson type: front crawl body position
Level: adult or child intermediate
Previous learning: basic front crawl technique
Lesson aim: to improve basic front crawl body position and shape
Equipment: floats and/or kickboards

Exercise/Activity	Teaching Points	Organisation	Duration
Entry: swivel entry	enter slowly	all together	1 min
Warm up: 2 widths any stroke without using buoyancy aids	take your time	all together	3 mins
Main Theme: 2 widths full stroke front crawl	relax and stretch	all together	2 mins
push and glide with a float held in both hands	feet together, toes pointed	all together	3 mins
push and glide without buoyancy aids	hands over each other	waves	3 mins
push and glide, marking distance travelled	stretch out, point toes	one by one	4 mins
push and glide, adding leg kick	hands together, stretch	waves	3 mins
push and glide adding front crawl stroke	relax and stretch	waves	3 mins
Contrasting Activity: forward somersault from a push and glide	tuck chin on chest	2 or 3 at a time	3 mins
sitting dive through a submerged hoop	hands together	2 or 3 at a time	3 mins
Exit: using the pool steps or over the poolside	take your time	one by one	1 min

Total time: 29 minutes

Lesson #5 Assessment

Lesson Objective: to improve basic front crawl body position and shape.

Below average	Average	Above average
😐	🙂	😎
Attempts to demonstrate but does not show the correct technique	Able to perform most of the technique correctly some of the time	Performs the technique correctly most of the time

Assessment	😐	🙂	😎
Face is submerged whilst moving			
Body position is horizontal			
Feet are together with toes pointed whilst moving			
Hands are together with fingers together			
Hips are level whilst moving			
Shoulders are level whilst moving			

Lesson Plan #6

Lesson type: front crawl body position
Level: adult or child advanced
Previous learning: full stroke front crawl
Lesson aim: to develop and fine-tune front crawl body position and shape
Equipment: fins

Exercise/Activity	Teaching Points	Organisation	Duration
Entry: sitting or shallow dive entry	take your time	all together	1 min
Warm up: 2 lengths any stroke	steady pace	all together	3 mins
Main Theme: 1 length full stroke front crawl	relax and stretch	all together	2 mins
push and glide from the poolside	feet together, toes pointed	all together	3 mins
push and glide, adding leg kick	hands together, stretch out	waves	3 mins
Kicking on side using fins, one arm stretched out	keep head in a neutral position	one by one	3 mins
repeat above drill on opposite side	steady kick and stretch out	waves	3 mins
push and glide adding front crawl stroke	stretch and relax	waves	3 mins
Contrasting Activity: supine push and glide and rotate to prone position	keep head level	2 or 3 at a time	3 mins
front crawl and somersault mid swim	head down, chin to chest	2 or 3 at a time	3 mins
Exit: using the pool steps or over the poolside	take your time	all together	1 min

Total time: 28 minutes

Lesson #6 Assessment

Lesson Objective: to develop and fine-tune front crawl body position and shape.		
Below average	**Average**	**Above average**
😐	🙂	😎
Attempts to demonstrate but does not show the correct technique	Able to perform most of the technique correctly some of the time	Performs the technique correctly most of the time

Assessment	😐	🙂	😎
Face is submerged and head is level			
Body position is streamlined			
Body position remains streamlined whilst kicking			
Arms are stretched out and streamlined			
Hips and shoulders are level whilst moving			
Head remains in a neutral position whilst moving			

Lesson Plan #7

Lesson type: front crawl leg kick
Level: adult or child beginner
Previous learning: basic front paddle
Lesson aim: to learn basic front crawl leg kick and introduce breathing
Equipment: floats or kick-boards and buoyancy aids as necessary

Exercise/Activity	Teaching Points	Organisation	Duration
Entry: swivel entry	enter slowly	all together	1 min
Warm up: 2 widths any stroke using buoyancy aids	take your time	all together	3 mins
Main Theme: sitting the poolside demonstrating kicking action	pointed toes	all together	2 mins
holding the poolside and kicking	kick with straight legs	all together	3 mins
kicking with a float held under each arm	kick from the hips	one by one	4 mins
kicking with one float held in front	kick with floppy feet	teacher assisted	3 mins
holding the poolside blowing bubbles	blow gently	all together	2 mins
kicking with a float held under each arm adding blowing bubbles	kick and blow at the same time	all together	3 mins
Contrasting Activity: prone star float with or without a buoyancy aid	hold your breath	2 or 3 at a time	2 mins
supine star float with or without a buoyancy aid	relax and stay still	2 or 3 at a time	2 mins
Exit: using the pool steps	take your time	one by one	1 min

Total time: 26 minutes

Lesson #7 Assessment

Lesson Objective: to learn basic front crawl leg kick and introduce breathing.		
Below average	**Average**	**Above average**
😐	🙂	😎
Attempts to demonstrate but does not show the correct technique	Able to perform most of the technique correctly some of the time	Performs the technique correctly most of the time

Assessment	😐	🙂	😎
Toes are pointed			
Kick is alternating up and down			
Legs are together			
Kick comes from the hips			

Lesson Plan #8

Lesson type: front crawl leg kick
Level: adult or child intermediate
Previous learning: basic front crawl technique
Lesson aim: to strengthen and develop front crawl leg kick
Equipment: floats, kickboards, sinkers and hoop

Exercise/Activity	Teaching Points	Organisation	Duration
Entry: swivel or sitting dive entry	enter slowly	all together	1 min
Warm up: 2 widths any stroke	take your time	all together	3 mins
Main Theme: 2 widths full stroke front crawl	kick with long legs	all together	3 mins
kicking with one float held in front	kick from the hips	all together	3 mins
push and glide	Keep legs straight and feet together	one by one	4 mins
push and glide adding leg kicks	kick with feet together	one by one	4 mins
kicking with one float held vertically in front	kick with floppy feet	all together	2 mins
2 widths full stroke front crawl	kick with relaxed legs	all together	3 mins
Contrasting Activity: surface diving through a submerged hoop	hold your breath	2 or 3 at a time	2 mins
surface diving to retrieve sinkers	relax and stay still	2 or 3 at a time	2 mins
Exit: using the pool steps	take your time	one by one	1 min

Total time: 28 minutes

Lesson #8 Assessment

Lesson Objective: to strengthen and develop front crawl leg kick.		
Below average	**Average**	**Above average**
😐	🙂	😎
Attempts to demonstrate but does not show the correct technique	Able to perform most of the technique correctly some of the time	Performs the technique correctly most of the time

Assessment	😐	🙂	😎
Toes remain pointed whilst kicking			
Kick is relaxed and alternating			
Feet break the water surface			
Leg kick is rhythmical			

Lesson Plan #9

Lesson type: front crawl leg kick
Level: adult or child advanced
Previous learning: full stroke front crawl
Lesson aim: to develop and perfect front crawl leg kick
Equipment: fins and floats or kickboards

Exercise/Activity	Teaching Points	Organisation	Duration
Entry: sitting or shallow dive entry	take your time	waves	1 min
Warm up: 2 lengths any stroke	take your time	all together	3 mins
Main Theme: 1 length full stroke front crawl	kick with long legs	all together	3 mins
push and glide adding leg kicks	relaxed continuous kick	all together	3 mins
kicking with one float held vertically in front	kick with floppy feet	one by one	3 mins
vertical kicking using fins, remain upright, arms across the chest	kick from the hips	all together	3 mins
streamlined kicking using fins, arms out in front	continuous, steady kick	waves	3 mins
2 lengths full stroke front crawl	kick with relaxed legs	all together	3 mins
Contrasting Activity: push and glide into forward somersault	arms pull down to rotate	2 or 3 at a time	2 mins
supine push and glide into somersault	tuck chin to chest	2 or 3 at a time	2 mins
Exit: using the pool steps	take your time	waves	1 min

Total time: 27 minutes

Lesson #9 Assessment

Lesson Objective: to develop and perfect front crawl leg kick.		
Below average	**Average**	**Above average**
😐	🙂	😎
Attempts to demonstrate but does not show the correct technique	Able to perform most of the technique correctly some of the time	Performs the technique correctly most of the time

Assessment	😐	🙂	😎
Toes break the water surface			
Knees and ankles are relaxed			
Leg kick remains relaxed when added to the whole stroke			
Leg kick is rhythmical and in time with the arm action			

Lesson Plan #10

Lesson type: front crawl arms
Level: adult or child beginner
Previous learning: basic front paddle and submerging the face
Lesson aim: to introduce basic front crawl arm action
Equipment: floats, buoyancy aids as necessary

Exercise/Activity	Teaching Points	Organisation	Duration
Entry: swivel entry	enter slowly	all together	1 min
Warm up: 2 widths any stroke using buoyancy aids	take your time	all together	3 mins
Main Theme: standing the poolside demonstrating arm action	continuous smooth action	all together	2 mins
walking through the water using arms	Keep fingers together	waves	3 mins
single arm action with float held in one hand	elbow exits first	one by one	4 mins
repeat the above with the opposite arm	finger tips enter first	one by one	4 mins
front crawl catch up holding a float	reach over the surface	waves	3 mins
full stroke front crawl	continuous arm action	all together	3 mins
Contrasting Activity: push and glide (longest distance contest)	stretched out and long body	2 or 3 at a time	2 mins
supine push and glide	push your hips up	2 or 3 at a time	2 mins
Exit: using the pool steps	take your time	one by one	1 min

Total time: 28 minutes

Lesson #10 Assessment

Lesson Objective: to introduce basic front crawl arm action.		
Below average	**Average**	**Above average**
😐	🙂	😎
Attempts to demonstrate but does not show the correct technique	Able to perform most of the technique correctly some of the time	Performs the technique correctly most of the time

Assessment	😐	🙂	😎
Arm pulls are alternating			
Elbows bend with each pull			
Fingers are together			
Arms recover over the water surface			

Lesson Plan #11

Lesson type: front crawl arms
Level: adult or child intermediate
Previous learning: basic front crawl technique
Lesson aim: to progress basic front crawl arm action and introduce breathing
Equipment: floats, pull buoys and sinkers

Exercise/Activity	Teaching Points	Organisation	Duration
Entry: swivel entry	enter slowly	all together	1 min
Warm up: 2 widths full stroke front crawl	take your time	all together	3 mins
Main Theme: single arm action with float held in one hand	elbow exits first	one by one	4 mins
repeat the above with the opposite arm	finger tips enter first	one by one	4 mins
repeat single arm exercises with float, adding breathing technique	breathe to the pulling side	waves	3 mins
front crawl catch up holding a float	reach over the surface	waves	3 mins
front crawl arms only using a pull buoy	pull with power	waves	3 mins
full stroke front crawl	smooth arm action	all together	3 mins
Contrasting Activity: sitting dive	head tucked into arms	2 or 3 at a time	2 mins
surface dive and collect sinkers	head tucked down, eyes open	2 or 3 at a time	2 mins
Exit: using the pool steps	take your time	one by one	1 min

Total time: 29 minutes

Lesson #11 Assessment

Lesson Objective: to progress basic front crawl arm action and introduce breathing.		
Below average	**Average**	**Above average**
😐	🙂	😎
Attempts to demonstrate but does not show the correct technique	**Able to perform most of the technique correctly some of the time**	**Performs the technique correctly most of the time**

Assessment	😐	🙂	😎
Arm pulls are relaxed and alternating			
Elbows bend and exit the water first			
Finger tips enter the water first			
Arm recovery over the water surface is relaxed and controlled			
Arm pulls are continuous as a breath is taken			

Lesson Plan #12

Lesson type: front crawl arms
Level: adult or child advanced
Previous learning: full stroke front crawl
Lesson aim: to develop and fine-tune front crawl arm action
Equipment: fins, pull buoy, hand paddles

Exercise/Activity	Teaching Points	Organisation	Duration
Entry: sitting or shallow dive entry	take your time	waves	1 min
Warm up: 2 lengths full stroke front crawl	take your time	all together	3 mins
Main Theme: front crawl arms only using a pull buoy	continuous, smooth arms	waves	3 mins
using fins, single arm pull with opposite arm stretched out in front	finger tips enter first	waves	3 mins
repeat above drill with opposite arm	stretch then pull	waves	3 mins
using fins, front crawl catch up holding a float	reach over the surface	waves	3 mins
front crawl with hand paddles	pull with power	waves	3 mins
full stroke front crawl	smooth arm action	all together	3 mins
Contrasting Activity: front crawl to poolside and somersault	plant feet onto the poolside	2 or 3 at a time	3 mins
basic front crawl start	head tucked down on entry	2 or 3 at a time	3 mins
Exit: using the pool steps or over the poolside	take your time	waves	1 min

Total time: 29 minutes

Lesson #12 Assessment

Lesson Objective: to develop and fine-tune front crawl arm action.		
Below average	**Average**	**Above average**
😐	🙂	😎
Attempts to demonstrate but does not show the correct technique	Able to perform most of the technique correctly some of the time	Performs the technique correctly most of the time

Assessment	😐	🙂	😎
Arms pull under the body to the thighs			
Arm recovery is controlled and not rushed			
Hands enter inside the shoulder line and stretch forwards			
Arm recovery over the water surface is relaxed and controlled			
Elbow exists first			

Lesson Plan #13

Lesson type: front crawl breathing
Level: adult or child beginner
Previous learning: basic front paddle, submerging face and blowing bubbles
Lesson aim: to introduce basic front crawl breathing technique
Equipment: floats, buoyancy aids and sinkers as necessary

Exercise/Activity	Teaching Points	Organisation	Duration
Entry: swivel entry	enter slowly	all together	1 min
Warm up: 2 widths any stroke on the front	take your time	all together	3 mins
Main Theme: breathing while standing and holding poolside	blow slowly and gently	all together	2 mins
repeat the above, but rolling the head to the side	look to your shoulder	all together	2 mins
holding a float with a diagonal grip	blow through your mouth	waves	3 mins
single arm pull with float held in one hand	turn your head to the pulling arm	one by one	4 mins
repeat the above with the opposite arm	turn your head as your arm pulls	one by one	4 mins
full stroke front crawl	head returns to central	all together	3 mins
Contrasting Activity: head first surface dive to collect sinkers	dig yourself down to the bottom	waves	2 mins
prone star floats	take a deep breath	waves	2 mins
Exit: using the pool steps	take your time	one by one	1 min

Total time: 27 minutes

Lesson #13 Assessment

Lesson Objective: to introduce basic front crawl breathing technique.		
Below average	**Average**	**Above average**
🙂	🙂	😎
Attempts to demonstrate but does not show the correct technique	Able to perform most of the technique correctly some of the time	Performs the technique correctly most of the time

Assessment	🙂	🙂	😎
Head is in a central position			
Head is face down			
Exhalation is from the mouth			
Head rolls to the side			
Head turns to the arm pulling side			

Lesson Plan #14

Lesson type: front crawl breathing
Level: adult or child intermediate
Previous learning: basic front crawl technique
Lesson aim: to develop and progress front crawl breathing technique
Equipment: floats and/or kickboards

Exercise/Activity	Teaching Points	Organisation	Duration
Entry: swivel or sitting dive entry	enter slowly	waves/ all together	1 min
Warm up: 2 widths any stroke	take your time	all together	3 mins
Main Theme: 2 widths full stroke front crawl	slow and steady	all together	3 mins
holding a float with a diagonal grip	breathe out slowly	waves	3 mins
single arm pull with float held in one hand	one ear up, one ear down	waves	3 mins
repeat the above with the opposite arm	look at your shoulder	waves	3 mins
repeat the above, one width each arm, breathing with alternate arm pulls	steady, controlled breathing	waves	3 mins
full stroke breathing every 3 arm pulls	take your time	waves	3 mins
Contrasting Activity: treading water	ears above the water	all together	2 mins
head first sculling	look up at the sky	waves	3 mins
Exit: using the pool steps	take your time	one by one	1 min

Total time: 28 minutes

Lesson #14 Assessment

Lesson Objective: to develop and progress basic front crawl breathing technique.

Below average	Average	Above average
😐	🙂	😎
Attempts to demonstrate but does not show the correct technique	Able to perform most of the technique correctly some of the time	Performs the technique correctly most of the time

Assessment	😐	🙂	😎
Breath is taken at regular intervals			
Head rolls to the side enough for the mouth to clear the water surface			
Exhalation is slow and controlled			
Head rolls to the side as the arm pulls			
Head rolls back down without lifting			

Lesson Plan #15

Lesson type: front crawl breathing
Level: adult or child advanced
Previous learning: full stroke front crawl
Lesson aim: to develop and perfect front crawl breathing technique
Equipment: fins, pull buoy, floats and/or kickboard

Exercise/Activity	Teaching Points	Organisation	Duration
Entry: sitting or shallow dive entry	take your time	waves	1 min
Warm up: 2 lengths front crawl	take your time	all together	3 mins
Main Theme: 1 length full stroke front crawl, breathing every 3 arm pulls	slow and steady	all together	3 mins
full stroke with pull buoy, breathing every 3 arm pulls	look at your shoulder	waves	3 mins
single arm pull with float held in one hand, increase time interval between breaths	one ear up, one ear down	waves	3 mins
repeat the above with the opposite arm	breathe out slowly	waves	3 mins
using fins, front crawl catch up increasing time interval between breaths	steady, controlled breathing	waves	3 mins
full stroke breathing every 3 arm pulls	take your time	waves	3 mins
Contrasting Activity: front crawl to the wall, somersault and push off on the back	plan feet on the pool wall	waves	3 mins
basic front crawl start	push hard from the legs	waves	3 mins
Exit: using the pool steps or over the poolside	take your time	one by one	1 min

Total time: 29 minutes

Lesson #15 Assessment

Lesson Objective: to develop and perfect front crawl breathing technique.		
Below average	**Average**	**Above average**
😐	🙂	😎
Attempts to demonstrate but does not show the correct technique	**Able to perform most of the technique correctly some of the time**	**Performs the technique correctly most of the time**

Assessment	😐	🙂	😎
Breathing is bi-lateral*			
Head remains level when rolling to the side			
Exhalation is slow and controlled			
Inhalation takes place in time with the arm pull			
Head rolls back down in time with arm recovery			
Breathing takes place at regular intervals			

*bi-lateral breathing is not compulsory. Breathing only to one side may be preferred when swimming longer distances.

Lesson Plan #16

Lesson type: front crawl timing and coordination
Level: adult or child beginner
Previous learning: basic front paddle with submerging face
Lesson aim: to introduce a basic front crawl timing pattern
Equipment: floats, buoyancy aids and sinkers as necessary

Exercise/Activity	Teaching Points	Organisation	Duration
Entry: swivel entry	enter slowly	all together	1 min
Warm up: 2 widths any stroke on the front	take your time	all together	3 mins
Main Theme: push and glide from the poolside	keep hands and feet together	one by one	3 mins
push and glide holding a float, adding leg kicks	count your kicks '1,2,3,4,5,6'	waves	3 mins
alternate arm pulls holding float out in front	Count '1,2,3' each pull	waves	3 mins
front crawl 'catch up' (repeat above without a float)	continuous leg kick	waves	3 mins
push and glide adding kicks and then arm pulls	count your kicks	one by one	4 mins
full stroke front crawl	continuous arms and legs	all together	3 mins
Contrasting Activity: supine star floats	look up at the sky and stretch out	2 or 3 at a time	2 mins
submerge to collect sinkers	deep breath and relax	2 or 3 at a time	2 mins
Exit: using the pool steps	take your time	one by one	1 min

Total time: 27 minutes

Lesson #16 Assessment

Lesson Objective: to introduce a basic front crawl timing pattern.		
Below average	**Average**	**Above average**
😐	🙂	😎
Attempts to demonstrate but does not show the correct technique	Able to perform most of the technique correctly some of the time	Performs the technique correctly most of the time

Assessment	😐	🙂	😎
Leg kicks are regular and alternating			
Arm pulls are regular and alternating			
Legs continue kicking when arms are pulling			
Arms continue to pull when legs are kicking			

Lesson Plan #17

Lesson type: front crawl timing and coordination
Level: adult or child intermediate
Previous learning: basic timing technique
Lesson aim: to progress and develop previous learning of front crawl timing
Equipment: floats, pull buoys and hoop

Exercise/Activity	Teaching Points	Organisation	Duration
Entry: swivel or sitting dive entry	enter slowly	waves/ all together	1 min
Warm up: 2 widths any stroke	take your time	all together	3 mins
Main Theme: 2 widths full stroke front crawl	slow and steady	all together	2 mins
kicking holding a float in both hands	count your kicks in groups of 6	waves	3 mins
alternate arm pulls holding float out in front	count '1,2,3' each pull	waves	3 mins
arm pulls with pull buoy between the legs	continuous arms	waves	3 mins
push and glide, add arms pulls and leg kicks	continuous kicking	waves	3 mins
full stroke front crawl	let the stroke flow	waves	3 mins
Contrasting Activity: feet first surface dives through a submerged hoop	stretch up and sink	one by one	4 mins
feet first sculling	toes at the surface	waves	3 mins
Exit: using the pool steps	take your time	one by one	1 min

Total time: 29 minutes

Lesson #17 Assessment

Lesson Objective: to progress and develop previous learning of front crawl timing.		
Below average	**Average**	**Above average**
😐	🙂	😎
Attempts to demonstrate but does not show the correct technique	Able to perform most of the technique correctly some of the time	Performs the technique correctly most of the time

Assessment	😐	🙂	😎
Legs kick in a regular pattern, in time with the arm pulls.			
Arms pull in a regular pattern with the leg kicks			
Leg kicking pattern remains continuous			
Arm pull pattern remains continuous			

Lesson Plan #18

Lesson type: front crawl timing and coordination
Level: adult or child advanced
Previous learning: full stroke front crawl
Lesson aim: to develop and fine-tune front crawl timing
Equipment: fins and pull buoys

Exercise/Activity	Teaching Points	Organisation	Duration
Entry: sitting or shallow dive entry	take your time	waves	1 min
Warm up: 2 lengths front crawl	take your time	all together	3 mins
Main Theme: 1 length full stroke front crawl	slow and steady	all together	2 mins
using fins, swim slow motion front crawl	keep head level	waves	3 mins
using fins, steady pace front crawl	let the kicks balance the arm pulls	waves	3 mins
arm pulls with pull buoy between the legs	continuous arms	waves	3 mins
push and glide, add arms pulls and leg kicks	continuous kicking	waves	3 mins
full stroke front crawl	stay level and balanced	waves	3 mins
Contrasting Activity: swim front crawl to poolside and flip turn	twist and extend away	waves	3 mins
front crawl grab start	fast transition to stroke	waves	3 mins
Exit: using the pool steps	take your time	one by one	1 min

Total time: 28 minutes

Lesson #18 Assessment

Lesson Objective: to develop and fine-tune front crawl timing.		
Below average	**Average**	**Above average**
😐	🙂	😎
Attempts to demonstrate but does not show the correct technique	Able to perform most of the technique correctly some of the time	Performs the technique correctly most of the time

Assessment	😐	🙂	😎
Legs kick 6 kicks to each cycle of arm pulls			
Legs kick and arms pull in a continuous and regular pattern			
Regular timing pattern is sustained over longer distances			

"Now that you have finished my book, would you please consider writing a review? Reviews are the best way readers discover great new books. I would truly appreciate it."

Mark Young

For more information about teaching swimming, learning to swim and improving swimming technique visit **Swim Teach**.

Swim Teach
Teaching · Learning · Achieving · *Professional Swimming Help Online*

"The number one resource for learning to swim
and improving swimming technique."

www.swim-teach.com

www.ingramcontent.com/pod-product-compliance
Lightning Source LLC
Chambersburg PA
CBHW062048090426
42740CB00016B/3053